SENTINEL

ROGER AILES

ZEV CHAFETS is the author of twelve books of fiction, media criticism, and social and political commentary. He is a frequent contributor to *The New York Times Magazine* and a former columnist for the *New York Daily News*.

NONFICTION

Double Vision
Heroes and Hustlers, Hard Hats and Holy Men
Members of the Tribe
Devil's Night
A Match Made in Heaven
Cooperstown Confidential
Rush Limbaugh

FICTION

Inherit the Mob
The Bookmakers
The Project
Hang Time
Whacking Jimmy (as William Wolf)

ROGER AILES

OFF CAMERA

Zev Chafets

SENTINEL

SENTINEL
Published by the Penguin Group
Penguin Group (USA) LLC
375 Hudson Street
New York, New York 10014

USA | Canada | UK | Ireland | Australia | New Zealand | India | South Africa | China
penguin.com
A Penguin Random House Company

First published in the United States of America by Sentinel, a member of Penguin Group (USA)
Inc., 2013
This paperback edition published 2013

PHOTOGRAPH CREDITS
Insert page 4 (top): Richard Nixon Presidential Library and Museum
5 (top): George Bush Presidential Library and Museum
5 (bottom): AP Photo / Jennifer Graylock
6 (bottom): Patrick McMullan / PatrickMcMullan.com / Sipa USA
7 (bottom): Rob Kim / Getty Images Entertainment / Getty Images

THE LIBRARY OF CONGRESS HAS CATALOGED THE HARDCOVER EDITION AS FOLLOWS:
Chafets, Zev.
Roger Ailes / Zev Chafets.
pages cm
Includes index.
Summary: "An illuminating look at the life, politics, and practices of Roger Ailes, founder and
CEO of Fox News Channel. As a political consultant, he helped put Richard Nixon, Ronald Reagan,
and George H. W. Bush in the White House"—Provided by publisher.
ISBN 978-1-59523-095-9 (hc.)
ISBN 978-1-59523-108-6 (pbk.)
1. Ailes, Roger. 2. Businesspeople—United States—Biography. 3. Executives—United States—Bi-
ography. 4. Political consultants—United States—Biography. 5. Fox News. I. Title.
HC102.5.A35C43 2013
338.7′6179145092—dc23
[B]
2012039790

Printed in the United States of America
10 9 8 7 6 5 4 3 2 1

Designed by Sabrina Bowers

To Betty Chafets Miller, the Matriarch

CONTENTS

Roger Ailes looked across his desk at me and said, "Some people say that I'm simple, and some people say that I'm complex. What do you think?"

Good question. For months, Ailes and I had been meeting regularly at Fox News headquarters in midtown Manhattan, at his home in Putnam County, and at public and private gatherings. He allowed me to sit in on his meetings, introduced me to his family, and gave his inner circle the green light to talk to me. In that time I got a closer, more prolonged look at Roger Ailes than any journalist ever has. He was naturally curious about what I had concluded. Simple or complex?

The answer itself isn't simple. Ailes, in his years as a political consultant, created images for a living, and his own narrative is constructed from the sturdy materials of American mythology. In our first meeting, he said he had dug ditches as a kid and would be happy to go back to it if the whole media empire thing ever fell apart. Ailes is no more likely than I am to dig ditches (and a lot less likely to need to) but I got his point. He is a blue-collar guy from a factory town in Ohio who has stayed close to his roots. That day, and subsequently, I found him plainspoken, wryly profane, caustic, and anxious for me to know that he doesn't give a good goddamn about fancy parties, political correctness, or the esteem of the Manhattan media *bien-pensants*. After I had known him for a while I asked what he would do if he were president of the United States. He said that he would sign no legislation, create no new regulations, and allow the country to return to its natural, best self, which he locates, with modest social amendments, somewhere in midwestern America circa 1955. In 2011, he won a Horatio Alger Award, and said, "People who believe they can win will eventually win." What could be simpler than that?

Still, Ailes is not another working-class stiff who got ahead through hard work and the power of positive thinking. For fifty years, he has navigated the waters of show business, national politics, and big-time media. He taught Dick Nixon new tricks, stepped in as Reagan's emergency debate coach when the Great Communicator needed help communicating, and held George H. W. Bush's hand all the way to the White House. He more or less invented modern political consulting and made a small fortune along the way. When he left politics, he talked his way into the number one job at CNBC and then convinced Rupert Murdoch to gamble a billion dollars, give or take, on an idea and a handshake. The gamble became Fox News, one of the most lucrative and influential news organizations on the planet. The last time they met, Barack Obama, not a Fox News fan, called Ailes "the most powerful man in America." If a Machiavelli society gave an award, it would be on Ailes's mantel, next to the Horatio.

Writing about a man as wily and charming as Ailes is a challenging business, and from the outset we established ground rules. He cooperated with me, but the book is not authorized. I checked his quotes for accuracy (which is my practice in any case) but he had no control over the manuscript. When he said something was off the record (which he rarely did) it stayed off; everything else was fair game.

Ailes opened up Fox News, which is usually about as reporter-friendly as Teheran. I spent time with Fox executives and on-air personalities, toured usually off-limits venues, and spent many hours with Ailes himself. He was open with me, although I never thought he was telling me everything. He intends to write an autobiography someday, and I imagine he is holding something in reserve. The result, this book, is not a formal biography. It is a record of almost a year spent watching Roger Ailes in action.

My access came at a price. It always does. The dynamic between a writer and his subject, especially one as controversial and powerful as Roger Ailes, necessarily contains elements of mutual seduction and self-interest and sometimes mistrust. Ailes didn't want to be eviscerated by a reporter. I didn't want to get conned by a master image maker.

Roger Ailes has his admirers, some of them surprising, and his detractors—entire organizations dedicated to discrediting him and all his works. I talked to a great many people on both sides. But Ailes is the main character, and I have left him front and center, allowing him to speak for himself. Ailes is a fascinating man, full of contradictions and surprises. He has certainly transformed American media and political discourse. How has he done it? What will he do next? What stokes his competitive fires and occasional rages? How to reconcile his acts of exceptional loyalty and private generosity (even to rivals) with his impulse to present himself to the world as a nasty, ruthless leg breaker? What makes Roger run—and where, if anywhere, is the finish line? Is he, in the end, simple or complex? It remains an excellent question. As Ailes himself might say: I report, you decide.

ROGER AILES

ZAC'S GAME

In mid-January, Roger Ailes skipped out on his duties at Fox News to attend a basketball game. The contest featured his twelve-year-old son, Zac, who plays for his Upper East Side Catholic boys' school. On weekends, the Ailes family is in Cold Spring, New York, on the banks of the Hudson River, but Ailes doesn't like the education on tap in the local school, so they have taken a place in the city not far from Zac's school.

The gym was too small for bleachers, and the crowd too sparse to be a crowd. Just before game time, the only fans were Ailes, in a folding chair along the sideline and, at a discreet distance, his bodyguard, Jimmy Gildea, a retired New York City detective. A few more parents trickled in during the warm-ups. They nodded to Ailes in a friendly way, but didn't stop to chat. If they were surprised to find themselves sharing a moment with the head of Fox News, they didn't show it.

Ailes was dressed in his work clothes—black suit, starched white shirt, gold tie clip, and matching cuff links. His hair was slicked back and a pair of bifocals perched on his nose. The overall effect was that of a small-town banker in a Frank Capra movie. Ailes is past seventy and looks it, especially when he tries to walk on his bum leg. The other parents were young enough to be his children. But Zac is his only child, and perhaps the only person who could lure Ailes away from his office on a Wednesday afternoon. This was the third game of the season, and he had been there every time.

As we waited for the tip-off, Ailes ran down the roster. "Our guys," he called them. Zac was easily the tallest kid on the team, and when the action commenced, his father encouraged him to take advantage of it. "Don't get boxed out," he hollered. "Use your height. Hands up on defense!" He waved his own hands to demonstrate. Zac looked over at his father and nodded. He had heard this mantra often. When Ailes was around Zac's age, basketball was his game. He played at the Warren, Ohio, YMCA, where he compensated for his own lack of height with a competitive spirit and, thanks to his mother's insistence on lessons, a trained dancer's grace. He had been a decent point guard, but like any father he wanted his son to surpass him.

Zac hit the first shot of the game, and Ailes clapped loudly and shouted his approval. But Zac's team, wearing red, was no match for the other school. As they fell behind, Ailes grew tense, barking instructions at his son and the rest of the team, but the advice wasn't helping. Zac came out of the game and took a seat at the end of a bench, away from the coach. Ailes caught his attention and motioned for him to move over and get closer. The boy dutifully complied. That was better. Ailes relaxed and resumed cheering. He made a point of calling encouragement to all the players, not just his son. When the other team scored, he maintained a stoic silence or called out, "Never mind. Go get 'em, boys!"

Ailes's old-fashioned clothes and pugnacious attitude reminded me of Red Auerbach, the great Celtics coach whose teams won nine championships. But not even Auerbach ever dominated his game the way that Ailes does. The redhead won nine championships, but it took him thirty years; Ailes, who founded Fox News in 1996, was already on his tenth straight year as number one and he was well on his way to an eleventh. During a time-out he extracted his BlackBerry for a quick peek at the standings. "Let's see if Fox News is still on the air," he said. "He studied the screen for a moment and smiled. "Yeah, looks like we're okay. We beat CNN, CNBC, and MSNBC combined, in prime time and the twenty-four-hour cume."

Back on the court, Zac caught a stray elbow to the eye. "Shake it off," Ailes hollered. "Rub it out! Back on defense! Get all over them! Come on, fellas, show some heart!" But sometimes heart isn't enough. At the final buzzer the score was 29–10. The boys headed for the locker room, but Ailes motioned for Zac, who loped over. "You made a couple of mistakes out there," he told the boy. "You threw that one ball away. And you missed an open shot underneath." Zac nodded. "But," Ailes said more gently, "you did a lot of things right. You played hard. You hustled. You scored 20 percent of your team's points. And when you got hit you didn't whine." The boy smiled; meeting his father's standard of toughness is even more important than winning.

Ailes put his arm on Zac's shoulder. "I'm proud of you, son," he said. "Now, let's get you home. You have schoolwork to do." They walked out of the gym, Ailes's arm still around his son's shoulders. A black Lincoln was idling at the curb, waiting to drop Zac at home and take Roger Ailes back to the world where he can control the score.

CHAPTER ONE

WARREN

In 2008, Roger Ailes, the most illustrious son of Warren, Ohio, was invited to speak at the dedication of the Trumbull County Veterans Memorial near Courthouse Square. Fifteen hundred people—some of them carrying signs reading Come Back, Roger, and Bring Jobs—turned up to hear his nostalgic, patriotic speech.

Warren, Ohio, is a once great town, at least in the fond childhood memories of Roger Ailes. I have similar feelings about my own hometown, Pontiac, Michigan, another bustling industrial hub in the days of Ike and JFK, before the belt began to rust. Warren was an important town, the county seat, a place where every four years presidential candidates rolled through town in open touring cars, waving at the crowd. It had a grand courthouse, a thriving downtown full of movie palaces, self-important local banks, and even a fine restaurant, the Saratoga.

During the Civil War, Warren was a Yankee hamlet of less

than three thousand. But at the start of the twentieth century, things changed. Steel mills sprang up. Packard opened an automobile factory. There were jobs, and a flood of workers—Italian immigrants, white and black Southerners—to fill them. By the time Ailes was growing up there, in the forties and fifties, Warren's population was climbing toward sixty thousand. Today, it is closer to forty thousand.

Warren was more than manufacturing. It sits about halfway between Chicago and New York, which made it a stopping point on the booze highway during Prohibition—people sometimes called it "Little Chicago"—and it retained its raffish character after repeal. The Mafia became firmly established in the entire Mahoning Valley. Warren's politics were rough-and-ready. Perhaps the region's most famous statesman was Congressman Jim Traficant, who represented the valley for twenty years before getting busted on a bribery charge. He got a seven-year sentence, ran for reelection from his federal prison cell, and won 15 percent of the vote.

The Mafia was an irritant in Warren, but during World War II the Nazis posed what appeared to be a greater threat. The Mahoning Valley, with its steel mills, mines, and factories, saw itself as the American Ruhr, which the Allies were bombing into uselessness, and there was widespread concern that the Germans would try to retaliate. The first years of Roger Ailes's life were spent under blackout and curfew, enforced by air-raid wardens including Roger's father, Bob. National security concerns didn't dissipate after the fall of the Third Reich. During the Cold War, American kids everywhere were drilled on ducking under their desks in the event of an atomic attack, and the threat was taken with special seriousness in places like Warren (and in Pontiac). "People figured that as soon as the Russian missiles headed south across the Canadian border they would be aimed right at us," Ailes recalls.

Paranoia and civic pride coexisted in Warren, Ohio, during the Eisenhower years. The factories were hiring and at peak production. A Chamber of Commerce report, issued in 1955, declared Warren "well balanced industrially, with a great diversification of products from basic steel to finished consumer items. Endowed with a great deal of natural resources and strategically located between Cleveland and Pittsburgh, the future of Warren is assured."

Young Roger Ailes was exposed to the typical diet of midwestern media. As a boy he delivered the *Youngstown Vindicator*, a morning newspaper. "I used to go out at 5:00 a.m.," he recalls. "It was dark as hell, and freezing in the winter. On the way out of the house, my dad would give me a chocolate bar and I'd stop halfway through the route, duck into a storefront to get out of the wind, eat that candy, and then do the rest of the route." There was also a 5,000-watt AM radio station that featured local news and sports, and, due to the town's fortuitous location, six TV stations out of Youngstown, Pittsburgh, and Cleveland, all of which offered the same homogenized network "news from nowhere."

The main entertainment in Warren was downtown, at theaters like the Robbins—old-fashioned movie houses where the owner and his wife would personally greet the patrons with a handshake on Friday nights. Ailes was a movie buff who especially loved John Wayne westerns, army movies like *From Here to Eternity*, and patriotic fare such as *Yankee Doodle Dandy*, starring Jimmy Cagney. He was close to his maternal grandmother, and they would often take in a movie, save half their popcorn, and then, after the show, feed it to the squirrels near the courthouse fountain.

■ ■ ■

Roger Ailes was the middle child of Bob and Donna Ailes, an ill-matched couple with strong personalities and very different ideas about child rearing. Bob grew up in Warren, raised by a single mother. His father, Roger's grandfather, was a medical doctor with an additional degree in public health and a law school diploma to boot. Young Dr. Ailes went off to World War I and was killed in combat. That, at least, was the story his son grew up on. In fact, the story was less heroic. Dr. Ailes met a nurse in the army and never came home. He moved to Akron, fifty miles away, where he became a prominent physician. His abandoned wife was so bitter that she kept his existence a secret from everyone, including his son.

Bob Ailes grew up poor and working class, a displaced person in the social order of his small town. He found work at the Packard plant and became a foreman—a step up from the line, but far from the expectations of the son of a doctor. At twenty-nine he married Donna Cunningham, a local beauty queen ten years his junior. They had three children—Robert Jr. (known as "Rob"), Roger, and Donna Jean (called "Jeannie")—at three-year intervals. Bob was thirty-three when Roger was born.

Bob Ailes was a gregarious man. He called everyone "son" because he had trouble remembering names, but he was well liked and, within his own social realm, clubbable. He became a 32nd degree Mason, served as past Master of the Ali Baba Grotto of the Shriner's lodge, and was a freelance ward heeler for local politicians. He was also a hard worker who supplemented his income painting houses and expected his sons to pitch in. Outwardly he seemed like a guy who took life as it came, says Rob Ailes, Roger's older brother, but inwardly he seethed with resentment.

"One time I visited my father at work and saw him getting dressed down by some college boy executive at work," Roger recalls. "I asked him why he was taking that kind of shit. I remember exactly what he said. He said, 'I'm taking the guff so that someday you will be one of the guys giving the orders.'" Bob Ailes was young Roger's hero, and the humiliation made a deep impression. It is one of life's satisfactions that, as head of Fox News, he has some six thousand people reporting to him, including quite of lot of college boys.

Roger remembers his father with admiration as a man's man with an explosive temper. "One time we were in the car and a guy in a truck cut us off and gave my mother the finger," he told me. "My dad caught up with him at a stoplight, got over to the car, dragged the guy through the open window, and kicked his ass." But often the anger was directed at his children. "When he got mad, he beat me," says Ailes in a matter-of-fact tone. "He used an electric cord, a belt, whatever was handy."

"Spare the rod and spoil the child" was standard parenting back then, but Roger Ailes was not a standard child. He suffered from hemophilia. It made life precarious. Even minor injuries could set off unstoppable bleeding. When Roger was still a preschooler, he bit his tongue and almost died. "Blood was dripping out of his mouth like an icicle," recalls his brother. There was nothing that could be done in Warren, so Bob Ailes put him in the family car and raced to the Cleveland Clinic, sixty miles northwest, where doctors managed to stanch the bleeding and save Roger's life. Bob Ailes's coworkers from Packard came to the clinic to donate blood. "Always remember," Bob Ailes told his son, "you've got blue collar in your veins."

"Roger was always hurting himself," says his brother. "One time he fell off the fence and his arm swelled to about four times its usual size. Another time he was riding his bike, plowed through an intersection, and wound up in the hospital with internal bleeding. This was before immunization, so between the usual childhood contagious diseases and the hemophilia, he missed a lot of school." Their grandmother kept a diary, and in it she noted that Roger had received eighty-five injections in one three-week stint in the hospital. His body turned purple. "That's a lot of shots for a little kid," Ailes says.

Many men would have treated a boy like Roger with extreme caution. Bob Ailes didn't do that. He wanted his son to live a normal life, and in a place like Warren, Ohio, that meant being tough. "Dad never cut Roger any slack because of his illness," says Rob Ailes. "Maybe he felt guilty about the bruises and the welts when he was done beating us, maybe it worried him later on that he had done it, I don't know. We didn't talk about it. It seemed natural. Today he would go to jail for something like that, and we would have wound up in foster care."

In second grade, Roger was hit by a car. He didn't bleed out, but his legs were badly injured. Bob Ailes did not intend to have a cripple for a son. He took Roger out to the Warren G. Harding High School track and told him to start running. "They had been using the track as a fairgrounds and it was covered with horseshit," says Ailes. "I pointed that out to my father and he said, 'Don't fall down and you won't get any on you.'"

Bob Ailes was a hard man, no doubt, but he was also capable of unexpected kindness. As a teenager Roger took out the family car—a very considerable privilege—and crashed it. "I came home scared to tell my old man," he recalls. "He was sitting in the living room reading the newspaper when I walked in, and I had to just spit it out."

"Are you hurt?" Bob Ailes asked without putting down the paper.

"No."

"Is anyone hurt?"

"No."

"A car is just a thing. We can fix it," said Bob Ailes. That was the end of the matter. More than fifty years later, Ailes tells the story with a mixture of relief and amazement.

"I think Roger was in denial about his disease," says Rob Ailes, who is a doctor. "It's very well known in the medical literature that hemophiliacs tend to be daredevils, the kind of guys who wind up jumping over canyons on motorcycles. Roger fit that bill. He was like a child diabetic who didn't want to take his medicine. He challenged life."

As a young kid, Roger got into a lot of fights, and he didn't mind taking on bigger kids. In junior high school he went out for football. His mother thought it was crazy, but Bob Ailes gave his son permission to play. By that time, Roger and he had an extremely close relationship. "He let Roger make his own restrictions," says Rob. "As he got older, Roger realized himself what he could and couldn't do." He quit football when he saw how dangerous it was, but he didn't stop taking chances. On a Boy Scout trek through Canada, he and some friends jumped into a river and saved a couple whose canoe had capsized.

These exploits didn't make Donna Cunningham Ailes happy. She didn't want her sons to grow up to be roughnecks. Her father, a pious Pentecostal Christian, migrated to Warren from West Virginia. Her parents never even made it to high school, and she had social and cultural aspirations for her children. Bob Ailes, no matter his current place, was a doctor's son. When her father died, Donna left the Pentecostal church for the more socially established First Presbyterian Church, an impressive structure located on Warren's "Millionaires' Row." She saw to it that the Ailes children had elocution and piano lessons, and the boys sometimes played duets in church. When Roger injured his legs, her idea of rehab was forcing him to take ballet and tap dance classes with his sister, an indignity for which he has yet to forgive her. To finance all this self-improvement, Donna made lace doilies and embroidered hankies that the Ailes children sold door-to-door, much to their chagrin.

Bob Ailes was indifferent to his sons' school performance; Donna was a different story. She demanded good grades. Rob, the dutiful son, obliged with straight A's and an acceptance to Oberlin College. Roger wasn't interested. "He wouldn't play her game," says Rob. "He was the creative type, and they didn't give grades for that. Kids like him were considered lazy or stupid. But he didn't care. His attitude was, the hell with it, I don't need these classes and I don't give a damn about grades. He wouldn't budge and eventually he forced our mother to compromise."

When Roger finished high school, his father took him aside and told him that he would have to leave. "Go out and get a job. Join the service. Or if you want to go to college, for every dollar you put up, I'll try to match it with a dollar," he said. Roger was shocked and hurt. He thought he was being cast out as a further lesson in Bob Ailes's tough love. But he was mistaken. This was part of a larger family drama he didn't fully grasp.

Roger decided to go to college at Ohio University. It was cheap, it had a reputation as a party school, and he could get in with less than stellar grades. His parents drove up to Athens and dropped him off. When he came home for Christmas break, he found his house sold and his belongings discarded. His mother had gone west with Joe Urban, a New York reporter turned fund-raiser for the American Cancer Society whom she met at a convention. "My mother was what you could call self-absorbed," says Rob. "She did what suited her."

Bob Ailes fell into a deep depression and moved in with his own mother. Seeing him that way was shocking, but Roger tried not to take sides. "They both had a case," he says. "My dad was ten years older, a factory guy, and she was very smart and very stylish. And he had a temper. Joe was a sweet man. I didn't blame anyone for anything." In 1989, Ailes wrote his only book, a how-to communication guide titled *You Are the Message*, and dedicated it to his wife, his mother, and Joe Urban.

Ailes, homeless, spent his freshman winter break at the home of his best friend, Doug Webster, who was on his way to becoming a naval aviator and who died a few years later, during the Vietnam War, in the Sea of Japan. When Roger left Warren, after the New Year, it was for good.

■ ■ ■

The first time I met Roger Ailes we talked about his child-hood and he mentioned Doug Webster and what a blow it had been to lose him. And he talked about another old friend, still very much alive but, as far as Ailes knew, gone forever. Austin Pendleton was a scion of one of Warren's wealthier families. His mother, Frances Manchester Pendleton, was an amateur actress who belonged to a local theatrical company. "Austin and I were very close friends," Ailes recalled. "We used to play together in his backyard, which was on a stream, and we had sleepovers at one another's houses." In junior high school, Pendleton formed a theater company of his own, and Ailes sometimes appeared in the shows. "Austin was a natu-ral talent," Ailes told me. "He went to Yale and became a re-ally great actor and director. I miss him."

"What happened to him?" I asked.

"I hear he lives in New York, but I haven't seen him in years," Ailes said. "I imagine his friends think I'm the devil. I wouldn't want to embarrass him by getting in touch."

I went home and Googled "Austin Pendleton," who was, indeed, alive and well and living in New York. He had appeared in more than thirty movies—in his first, *Skidoo*, he shared a memorable scene with Groucho Marx, in a rowboat on the Pacific Ocean smoking a joint—and dozens of plays on and off Broadway. He directed Elizabeth Taylor and Maureen Stapleton in Lillian Hellman's *Little Foxes* at the Martin Beck Theatre (now the Al Hirschfeld) and taught acting at the HB Studio in New York and directing for a few years at the New School. Roger was right: his old playmate was at the heart of the progressive artistic community of Manhattan.

I sent Pendleton an e-mail, telling him I was working on a book about Ailes and asking if he would be willing to talk to me. He replied immediately. "I certainly will. Roger is a fascinating, wonderful character in my life."

Ailes was surprised and pleased to hear that he was still in the good graces of his old pal. He invited Austin to come by Fox for lunch. I ran into Pendleton in the lobby, where he was being chatted up by an earnest young actor. Pendleton is small and very thin, with a crown of unkempt white hair, and was dressed in a plaid work shirt, faded jeans, and boots, one of which lacked a lace. Ailes was waiting for us in a private dining room on the third floor. They embraced warmly and began, as long-separated childhood friends do, by sizing up each other's physical condition. They assured each other that they had never looked better. Ailes patted his stomach and explained that he could no longer exercise after once again having wrecked his leg, this time in a skydiving incident in California. "I had a hip replaced and I guess I should again, but I think I'll just hang on to this one until I'm finished," he said.

Pendleton nodded sympathetically, although he looked like he could run a marathon. A waiter appeared. Ailes often dines on tuna sandwiches and potato chips at working lunches, but this time he laid on a feast of butternut squash soup and a choice of entrees.

They felt each other out with a series of anecdotes about the lives they had led since Warren. Ailes recounted a dinner party he had recently attended with Shirley MacLaine and Al Pacino. "He just stared at me the whole time. Probably invited me to see what a real, live conservative looks like up close," he said. It was an opening for Pendleton but he didn't take it.

"He does that with everyone," Pendleton assured him. "He just studies people. It can be disconcerting."

"Very strange," Ailes said. It seemed to me that Pendleton had left Ailes's implicit question—if he was considered persona non grata in the actor's world—unanswered. So I asked, "Are you embarrassed to tell your friends that you know Roger?"

"Not at all," said Pendleton. "I've been dining out on it for years. Everyone is very curious."

"I bet," Ailes said, but he sounded pleased.

Pendleton asked what it had been like working for Nixon. "I actually felt sorry for him," Ailes said. "His dad was brutal to him. He was ugly and awkward. By the time I met him, he had the 1960 election stolen from him by Kennedy, so he was a little bit paranoid, and somewhat weird. He once told me that the hardest part of being president was coming down to breakfast in the morning and explaining the horrendous cartoons Herblock did of him in the *Washington Post* to his daughters."

Pendleton offered a recollection of his own, a raunchy backstage encounter at a Washington theater between Liz Taylor, Lillian Hellman, Ronald and Nancy Reagan, and actress Maureen Stapleton that ended with the punch line "She fucked Max!" Ailes burst into laughter. Here they were, two guys from Warren, swapping tales about presidents and movie stars. But, more than a reunion of old friends, it seemed to me like a rare meeting between Ailes and the ghost of Roger past. He was hungry for memories of his own boyhood, and delighted when Pendleton recalled the mock election in a long-forgotten civics class.

"I was for Stevenson," he said, "until I heard Roger's speech for Eisenhower. I can still remember what you said. He was so informed and lucid, he knew so much, he made me want to switch to Ike."

"I figured a guy who had organized the invasion of Europe was probably qualified to be president," said Ailes. "I'm surprised it made an impression. You were mostly interested in putting on shows. I remember your mom used to pick the plays, but at a certain point you would just take over, tell everybody what to do and where to stand and how to act."

"She was a good producer," said Pendleton.

"Watching her cast those shows had a big influence on how I pick talent. And, you know, I produced some plays when I got to New York."

"*The Hot l Baltimore*," said Pendleton. "You won some awards for that one, right?"

Ailes nodded. *The Hot l Baltimore* won three Obies between 1973 and 1976, as well as a New York Drama Critics' Circle Award for Best American Play of 1973. "Long time ago," he said. "You know what I miss, Austin? I miss those days back in Warren. Sometimes I can close my eyes and see my family after church, my grandfather saying a prayer before

Sunday dinner. It's like that Kris Kristofferson song," Ailes said, "the one Janis Joplin recorded. 'I'd trade all my tomorrows for a single yesterday.' I still feel that way. . . ."

The door of the small private dining room flew open, and there stood Rupert Murdoch. He had been in the news lately, flying back and forth to London trying to put out the fires ignited by accusations of bribery and illegal hacking by his tabloid *News of the World*. It hadn't gone well. Murdoch's son James had just stepped down from control of the British newspaper operations, and Murdoch himself had been questioned by a public inquiry committee. He had looked old and a little confused in that appearance, but he seemed fresh now, trim and full of energy. He gave Pendleton and me a firm handshake, although he clearly had no idea who we were.

"Well, Roger, I just stopped in to say hello," he said. "Saw a great-looking woman, by the way, when I came in this morning. Never saw her before. Wonder who she was?"

Ailes asked what time he had seen her. "About nine thirty, I should think. She left the building carrying a garment bag."

"Must be the girl who reads the news on *Imus*," said Ailes. "She was with him on the radio. She wanted to do television, too, so I decided to give her a shot."

"Beautiful woman," said Murdoch. "Well done."

Ailes didn't seem particularly interested; Fox is loaded with former beauty queens. "You going to be around?" he asked.

"Off to London again for a week and then on to the Far East," Murdoch said. "You can reach me if something important comes up." He nodded to Pendleton and me and closed the door.

"Rupert is a very interesting guy," Ailes said. "He's grateful to me because I don't need anything. Sometimes he drops by and plops down on the couch and we make each other laugh.

When this crap in London started, he asked me if we had anything like that going on here."

A very good question, I thought. Pendleton looked like he thought so, too.

"I told him there's nothing here that's a problem," Ailes said. "Nothing at all. We don't do crooked things here—bug conversations and bribe police. That's not part of our culture."

"Of course not," said Pendleton. "We're from Warren, Ohio. We weren't raised that way." I couldn't tell if he was being sincere or not. He's an actor, after all.

Talk circled back to the old days. Ailes was glad to know that the theater company founded by Pendleton's mother is still putting on plays. He confessed that he doesn't get back to Warren often; that speech to the Veterans Memorial had been his last visit. "I used to go back when my father was alive," he said. "You know, he remarried."

Pendleton didn't know. Bob Ailes wasn't part of his family's social circle.

"We'd go out to dinner. My dad always ordered the same thing, a shrimp cocktail and a steak. He never had anything else. Then one time we went out to dinner at a place downtown, and when the waitress handed him a menu, he just looked at it blankly. He didn't remember what he liked to eat. His wife had to order for him. And he always planted tomatoes in the yard, and that year he stopped."

"How old was he?" asked Pendleton.

"Seventy-one," said Ailes. The same age as Austin Pendleton. The same age as Ailes himself. "You know, my dad's wife was a nice lady, but he never stopped loving my mother. When the Alzheimer's really took over, the only name he would say was 'Donna.' The last time I came to see him I told him, 'I love you, Dad,' but he didn't respond. I felt at the time that he would have wanted me to kill him and I considered it, but I couldn't. When I left him the last time I said, 'Don't worry, Dad, Donna will be up in heaven. You'll see her there.'"

We adjourned to Ailes's office on the second floor, where he showed Pendleton photos of his wife and son and promised to stay in touch. "I've missed you, old friend," he said, and the two men embraced. A secretary showed Pendleton out. Ailes looked out his window at Sixth Avenue for a long moment. Eight senior news executives were waiting for him in a nearby meeting room to go over the daily news budget. Ailes walked into the room and took his place at the head of the table, a man who sure as hell didn't plan to stop planting any goddamn tomatoes.

CHAPTER TWO

THE MIKE DOUGLAS SHOW

When Roger Ailes returned to the campus of Ohio University after Christmas break his freshman year, he was disoriented and demoralized. His life in Warren had been wiped away, his family dispersed or sunk in depression, his personal belongings carted away. And Athens, Ohio, didn't offer much in the way of distractions or stimulation. The town was a third of the size of Warren. The university, whose eight thousand students were mostly drawn from eastern Ohio, were there for an affordable, attainable, no-frills education. The school was intentionally dull and conventional. A promotional film of the time assured parents of prospective students that OU was dedicated to change, but not the kind of change "that is the result of uncertainty or willful experimentation."

The university boasted 285,000 volumes in its main library, but there is no indication that Roger Ailes troubled them much. He decided to become a fighter pilot, like his best friend, Doug Webster, and enrolled in the Air Force

ROTC, but he washed out because of his medical record. He decided to major in radio and television studies because of his theatrical background. He worked for two years as station manager of WOUB, the campus radio station, and got on-air experience doing play-by-play of Ohio University football. He also opened the station every morning and hosted *Yawn Patrol* in tandem with a blind fellow student, Don Matthews.

Ailes had gotten his first job at the station after receiving a tip from the station manager's girlfriend, Marjorie White, that a position had opened up. He and Marjorie met at a church event on campus—she was a senior majoring in art; he was still a freshman. At the time, he was feeling lonely and confused by his parents' abrupt split-up and he was drinking too much. Marjorie may have looked to him like a solution. He was impressed by her kindness and maturity and struck by the fact that she had been born and raised in Parkersburg, West Virginia. "My mother was born in Parkersburg," he told me. "She's the only other person I ever met from there. Hell, I don't want to get too psychological, but it was an interesting coincidence."

Marjorie White found Roger interesting, too. She broke up with her boyfriend, and they became a couple. By this time, the ex-boyfriend was also Ailes's boss, which was, he recalls, "awkward," but not a deal breaker. The couple were married in a small chapel near the campus during his junior year. She took a job teaching art while he finished his degree in fine arts.

In 1961, KYW-TV in Cleveland launched a daytime variety show hosted by a little-known song-and-dance man, Mike Douglas. The idea for the show came from Woody Fraser, a young producer at NBC's Chicago affiliate. "I watched a lot of daytime TV at the time, and it was very boring. I came up with the idea of an afternoon talk show with a regular host and, every week, a big-name cohost, a program that could be syndicated to stations around the country," Fraser says. He sold the concept to Westinghouse Broadcasting, which sent him to Cleveland to get it started. One of his first jobs was to select a host, and he wasn't exactly overwhelmed by big names who wanted a low-paying gig on an experimental show out of Cleveland. Some of the candidates showed up for auditions drunk. Others had prickly personalities that didn't appeal to a daytime audience. Douglas was handsome in a conventional way, affable and keen, and he got the job of a lifetime. The show ran in national syndication for more than twenty years.

The Mike Douglas Show started out as a lean operation. It aired five times a week, ninety minutes each day, and it had an initial staff of six. One of them was Launa Newman, a graduate of Northwestern University, who had gone to high school with Roger. Newman knew that Ailes had majored in television and was looking for a job, and she recommended him to Fraser, who invited Ailes to come in for an interview. Newman told him to bring one hundred show ideas with him, which he did.

"The ideas were good and I told him, 'You're frigging hired,'" says Fraser. "He started as a segment producer. It was the best hire I've ever made."

Fraser was a demanding and abrasive boss, and he was aware that the show's pace was taking a toll on the personal lives of its personnel. Marjorie and Roger lived in Cleveland, but he spent almost all of his time at the station. At one point Marjorie Ailes came to see Fraser to complain. "You're ruining my life with these crazy hours," she said. Fraser was unsympathetic. "I liked Marjorie," he says. "She was very attractive and smart; she looked like the actress Jeanne Crain. For that matter, Roger was handsome back then. Good-looking couple. And she was right: Roger didn't have much time for her. We basically worked from nine in the morning until eleven at night. That was the job. We did eight segments in every show, and I didn't let anybody go home until they were all finished."

Ailes impressed Fraser—and Fraser's boss Chet Collier—with his moxie and instinctive understanding of what made for good TV. "Look, it was easy to book Muhammad Ali back then [Ali, whose license was suspended, was out of boxing at the time], but it was a lot harder to do something interesting with him," says Fraser. "We came up with the idea of getting him to stage a mock fight with Robert Goulet. Roger saw that it was a good idea, but he wanted to know the dynamic—what was the premise? *Why* would Ali fight a singer, what would the point be, where were the laughs. And he was able to put this together in a way that really worked."

Bowling was hot in the early sixties, and a representative of Brunswick suggested a segment on how to do it. Ailes liked the idea, but Fraser thought it would work only if there was a regulation lane. The next morning he came to work and found a truck in front of the studio. "Roger came up to me and said, 'I got you the goddamn bowling lane.' That sounds nuts, but it is what you have to do if you want to interest viewers and keep them. Roger and I fought sometimes—he called me a slave driver and an asshole—but we kept adding stations."

Not all of Ailes's stunts worked. He booked a man who had twenty piranhas that devoured ham hocks. Fraser was skeptical, but Ailes promised that it would work as advertised. The day of the show, he began to worry, and decided to test it out with a trial run. The fish ate Ailes's ham hocks. But they didn't repeat the stunt when on the show. "Nothing happened," Fraser recalls. "Roger had killed their damn appetite."

Fraser was a hell-raiser, and he liked rowdy games. He often challenged the staff to office basketball, one-on-one.

Ailes didn't usually participate, but one day he agreed to play. He drove to the basket and Fraser, a towering man, hip-checked him into the corner of a desk. Suddenly Ailes stopped and sat down. "I've got this thing," he said. "It's a blood disease." He pulled down his pants and displayed a purple thigh. No one on the show had any idea that he was a hemophiliac. "It must have hurt like hell but he just went back to work," says Fraser. "He didn't even go home early that day, and he never mentioned it again."

In 1967, Woody Fraser received an offer to produce *The Dick Cavett Show*. Chet Collier, the head of Group W Productions, made Ailes executive producer of *The Mike Douglas Show*. Both Fraser and Collier would play important roles in Ailes's later career at Fox. But for now, he was twenty-five years old and in charge of the most successful afternoon show on television.

In August 1965, the Douglas show moved to Philadelphia. Marjorie and Roger set up housekeeping. She took a job in a bookstore; he maintained his fearsome work schedule.

"Roger Ailes was a legend at a very young age," says Marvin Kalb, who was a reporter at CBS News at the time. "His success at the Douglas show struck a chord. He was talked about in the seventies in New York, in television circles."

Ailes came out of Ohio with Middle American taste in entertainment. He loved meeting and working with old-time stars like Judy Garland, Liberace, Jack Benny, and Pearl Bailey. But the Douglas show kept up with the times, which, in the sixties, meant flirting with the counterculture. Ailes wasn't an immediate fan. "The Rolling Stones were on one time," he recalls. "When I first saw them, I thought they were no-talent shitheads. But then I heard them rehearse, and I realized that they were pretty good. They really worked hard, and I admire that." The Douglas show also became

known as a place that welcomed black artists. Ailes produced shows with James Brown, Dick Gregory, Ray Charles,
and Chuck Berry, to name a few. After the death of Dick
Clark, Aretha Franklin said that *American Bandstand* had
been important, but the place she really loved was *The Mike
Douglas Show*.

Barbra Streisand was just breaking out when she came to
Ohio to do a week as a guest host on the show. The gig paid
just $1,000. To sweeten the deal, Ailes booked her into a small
nightclub on the west side of Cleveland, where she appeared
with just a rhythm section. "There was a table to the right of
the stage that was really noisy," Ailes remembers. "One of the
loudest was a priest in a clerical collar. At one point, Streisand stopped in midsong and said, 'Shut the fuck up, Father,'
and then went back to the song." Forty years later, the scene
still makes Ailes laugh.

Another, less profane guest was Martin Luther King Jr.
"He came on three or four times," Ailes says. "He'd sit in my
office waiting to go on and we'd smoke cigarettes and chat
about personal things or what was happening politically. I really don't remember anything specific. I wish I could."

Bill Cosby was still an up-and-coming comic in 1964, when
he appeared on the Douglas show. Ailes and Woody Fraser
wanted him to do a weeklong stint as cohost, but Westinghouse balked. "I was told by a senior executive straight out,
'You can't put that nigger on the air. It will kill us in the
South,'" says Ailes. Cosby went on anyway, and the show
managed to survive almost twenty years. Ailes got a sense of
satisfaction from winning the fight with Westinghouse, and a
good anecdote to boot. "Back then I sometimes wrote comedy
sketches for the show," he recalls. "I wrote one about two
guys playing chess and what they were really thinking as the
game went on. A few years later I was watching *Hollywood*

Palace and damn if Cosby wasn't doing the bit. Not bad, getting a piece of comedy stolen by Bill Cosby."

Malcolm X was a little too far out of the mainstream for an afternoon variety show, especially after he applauded the assassination of John F. Kennedy as "chickens coming home to roost." But Ailes produced several interviews with Malcolm for a public affairs series on KTW. "The first time he came to the studio, he wouldn't even shake hands with me because I'm white," says Ailes. But after Malcolm performed the *hajj*, and broke with the Nation of Islam, he became less militantly antiwhite. When he came into the studio, he was pleasant and had his picture taken with Ailes. Six weeks later, he was assassinated in New York by Nation of Islam gunmen.

Forty years later, Ailes found himself at a banquet seated next to Congressman Elijah Cummings of Maryland. Cummings asked how an organization like the Congressional Black Caucus could sponsor a televised primary debate. Ailes suggested that the CBC and Fox News cosponsor one. The idea didn't go over well with many members of the Caucus, who viewed Fox as fundamentally hostile. Congresswoman Carolyn Kilpatrick of Detroit, the CBC chairwoman, was particularly skeptical about the wisdom of partnering with the enemy. Ailes met with her. She asked him to explain his sudden interest in civil rights. Ailes assured her that there was nothing sudden about it, and whipped out the picture with Malcolm. Kilpatrick was impressed, and the CBC and Fox jointly produced a Democratic primary debate in 2008, in Detroit.

As a producer, Ailes was constantly on the lookout for new guests. He spotted Dick Gregory at the hungry i club in San Francisco. Today Gregory is a sometimes contentious civil rights icon, but back then he was doing satire laced with borscht belt humor. "He was funny—'I bought a suit with two pairs of pants and burned a hole in the jacket'—and we booked him." He also worked with Richard Pryor, who walked off the set because he didn't like his billing on the show. "I chased him down Walnut Street and convinced him to come back," says Ailes. "He was temperamental, but he was a very talented guy."

In the midsixties, NBC had a rising star on *The Today Show*, Barbara Walters. As one of the first women in network news, she caught Ailes's eye. "Roger called the network and asked if I would be willing to go down to Philadelphia and do the Douglas show," she told me. She was and she did. In keeping with his philosophy of adding showmanship to his interviews, Ailes convinced her to perform gymnastics on the program with a Swedish tumbling team, a stunt that upset Walters's bosses in New York. "They thought it would hurt my reputation as a newswoman," she says. Luckily, she managed to survive and prosper, and the appearance was the beginning of a fifty-year friendship.

"Roger is a huge name and everybody knows who he is, but he doesn't strive for fame," she says. "He lives a quiet life. I was very happy when he finally married"—a reference to his latest marriage.

The Walters-Ailes friendship has been a matter of Manhattan gossip for years. "I dated Barbara a couple times, or took her out as an escort, but we never had an affair," Ailes told me. "We probably could have at some point, but we were always married or between marriages or talking about marrying someone. We never got beyond that point. But we trusted one another, and we still do."

■ ■ ■

In 1994, Roger Ailes established a scholarship program at Ohio University for broadcasting and journalism students.

After his success at Fox News, he donated half a million dollars to establish the Roger E. Ailes Newsroom at the school. In an interview with the campus radio station he was typically self-deprecating, wondering if they left his name on the place when he wasn't in Athens. A university press release quoted Ailes in less caustic terms: "Ohio University ignited my interest in broadcasting, which became my lifetime career," he said.

But it was *The Mike Douglas Show* that was Ailes's real alma mater. Woody Fraser taught him how to put on a show. From Douglas himself he learned "likability" and how to use it. And some of the lessons were provided by visiting guests.

One of the foundational Roger Ailes stories appears in his book, *You Are the Message*. He told it to me the first time we met, since he guessed—correctly—that I had yet to read the book myself. Bob Hope was a huge star; Ailes was a twenty-three-year-old assistant producer. The senior producers were all sick or away when Hope, in town to promote a book, unexpectedly decided to appear on the Douglas show.

Ailes was frazzled by the situation. One of his job-winning ideas for Fraser had been to get Bob Hope to sing and dance with Mike Douglas, and now here he was, accompanied by an entourage, in the studio, needing to make it happen. Hope was booked to do a five-minute plug. Ailes wanted him to stay for the entire ninety minutes but he was too scared to ask Hope. He was, he writes, "incoherent."

Hope took him by the shoulder and led him into the next room. "Kid, I know nothing about your show. I've never been on it and I don't know what you expect me to do. It's very important for you to speak up and tell people exactly what you want. I'm a big enough star to refuse whatever you request, if I decide to. But if I don't even know what you want, there's no way I can give it to you."

Ailes told Hope he wanted him to stay for the entire ninety minutes. "The network pays me $100,000 for that," Hope said, laughing. But he hit it off with Douglas and did stay. On the way out he turned to Ailes and said, "Next time, speak up."

CHAPTER THREE

POLITICS

Ailes spoke up when he met Richard Nixon.

In the autumn of 1967, Nixon was on the road in a quest to rehabilitate himself after losing the presidency in 1960 to John Kennedy and then, humiliatingly, the governorship of California to Pat Brown in 1962. After that loss, he conducted a spiteful press conference in which he promised reporters that they would no longer have Nixon to "kick around."

The landslide defeat of Barry Goldwater in the 1964 election opened the door for a comeback. The Republican right, led by Ronald Reagan, was stunned into disarray by the magnitude of the Goldwater debacle. New York governor Nelson Rockefeller, the great moderate hope, dithered until it was too late to mount an effective campaign for the nomination. Meanwhile, Nixon stumped the country raising money and accruing political debts from Republican candidates, which he cashed in for the top spot on the ticket.

During this barnstorming phase, Nixon came through

Philadelphia, where he was booked to appear on *The Mike Douglas Show*. He was still considered a has-been and, in sophisticated circles, something of a joke. Woody Fraser was at the studio when the former vice president arrived. "He was early and they brought him into my office," Fraser recalls. "I didn't know what to do with him. I mean, what the hell did I have to say to Richard Nixon? 'What have you been up to lately?'" Fraser said he was very sorry but he had a staff meeting to attend. Nixon asked if he could tag along. "I remember thinking, This guy was the vice president of the United States and he wants to come to a staff meeting of *The Mike Douglas Show*?" Fraser felt sorry for him, but not sorry enough to hang out. Says Fraser, "I asked Roger to take care of him, keep him happy and out of the way."

Ailes wasn't especially excited to meet Nixon. He may have spoken eloquently for Eisenhower in Miss Irwin's civics class, but he wasn't interested in politics. "I don't even know if I was registered to vote back then," he says. "We had Nixon on because we booked everybody. We had Little Egypt on the show that day. She was an exotic dancer who performed with a boa constrictor. I figured I better not put her and Nixon in the same greenroom. I didn't want to scare him, or the snake. So I stuck him in my office. If I had done it the other way around, I'd probably be managing snake dancers today."

It is also very possible that if Hubert Humphrey had turned up in the Douglas greenroom instead of Nixon, Ailes would have ended up working on the Democratic campaign in 1968. Ailes was far less political in those days than he was professionally ambitious.

The conversation between Ailes and Nixon has become a part of modern political lore. Nixon said that it was a shame a man couldn't get elected president without a gimmick like TV. Ailes assured him that the medium was here to stay. If

Nixon didn't grasp that, and figure out how to turn it to his advantage, he would never get to the White House.

It was a cheeky thing for a guy in his midtwenties to tell a two-term vice president of the United States. Nixon was, after all, making television history when Ailes was still in grade school. In the presidential campaign of 1952, a scandal over an alleged political slush fund threatened to cause Eisenhower to dump his running mate from the ticket. Nixon went on TV, still a new medium, and delivered a corny, emotional, and highly effective self-defense invoking his wife's "respectable Republican cloth coat" and his daughter's love for Checkers, the family dog. Another memorable moment came in 1959, when Nixon toured the American National Exhibition in Moscow and, standing in a model American kitchen with TV cameras running, debated Soviet ruler Nikita Khrushchev on the respective merits of communism and capitalism.

The 1960 presidential debates were what soured Nixon on TV. Nixon went into the first debate unprepared and without makeup. Kennedy was tanned, rested, and ready. People who heard the debate on the radio thought Nixon won, but television viewers saw the charismatic Kennedy completely outshine the untelegenic vice president. TV went from being a form of communication he manipulated to one he dreaded. Ailes was a cocky young guy who knew, he said, how to make Nixon shine on the screen. A few days after their meeting in Philadelphia, Leonard Garment, Nixon's law partner and confidant, invited Ailes to come up to New York for a meeting with the Nixon media team. "It was a Sunday morning," says Ailes. "We had breakfast at the Plaza Hotel and they grilled me for four hours. I guess they liked what they heard. They offered me a job producing Nixon's TV." Ailes took it. Mike Douglas was furious about losing his executive producer. Friends in the business thought Ailes was crazy to abandon a promising career for a flier with Tricky Dick. But he had a vision of what he could accomplish.

The result was the Man in the Arena campaign. Nixon wouldn't debate his Democratic opponent, Hubert Humphrey, or Alabama governor George Wallace, who was running as a third-party candidate. He would also keep his spontaneous public appearances to a minimum. Instead, Ailes staged a series of town meetings with selected audiences and prescreened citizen questioners who lacked the guile (and, in many cases, hostility) of the political press. Man in the Arena made it possible for Nixon to control his media environment. Ailes's role as a profane, skydiving, hard-charging producer was documented in *The Selling of the President*, a bestseller by Philadelphia columnist (and Ailes pal) Joe McGinniss.

Contrary to myth, Ailes did not win the election for Nixon. The country was in turmoil over Vietnam; there was racial violence in cities across America; Martin Luther King Jr. and Bobby Kennedy were murdered. President Lyndon Johnson was so unpopular that he decided not to run for reelection. It would have taken a much more compelling candidate than Vice President Hubert Humphrey to salvage the situation for the Democrats.

History recalls the 1968 campaign as the start of the Republican "Southern Strategy" of wooing conservative white Democrats below the Mason-Dixon Line. But it didn't quite work at the time, although it would when Ronald Reagan came along. Nixon carried only five Southern states that had traditionally gone Democratic (South Carolina, Florida, Virginia, North Carolina, and Tennessee). Humphrey got Texas. Wallace won the rest of the old Confederacy. Even if Humphrey had won Nixon's Southern states, he wouldn't have had a sufficient margin for election. George Wallace, running well to the right of Nixon, got forty-six electoral votes in the Deep South.

Ailes downplays his role in the Nixon victory. "People think I invented strategy or ads," he says. "Really, I was just the TV producer. I was in charge of making sure the backlights worked." It is an overly modest assessment. Ailes didn't win the election, but his careful handling and attention to detail in the staging of the Man in the Arena format helped make sure that Nixon didn't blow another election on TV.

After the victory, Ailes was hired as an outside adviser to the president. He was too young to be personally close to Nixon, and his advice could be abrasive. He once told Nixon not to ditch his wife when he left Air Force One and greeted reception committees. "Leaving her on the steps of the plane doesn't look too good on TV," he said.

Ailes wasn't really trusted by the Nixon inner circle. Some Nixonites blamed Ailes for the access McGinniss got and the unflattering observations Ailes made about the candidate. "Let's face it, a lot of people think Nixon is dull," McGinniss quoted Ailes as saying. "Think he's a bore, a pain in the ass. They look at him as the kind of kid who always carried a book bag. Who was forty-two years old the day he was born. They figure other kids got footballs for Christmas, Nixon got a brief-case and he loved it. He'd always have his homework done and he'd never let you copy. . . . Now you put him on television and you've got a problem right away. He's a funny-looking guy . . . [he] looks like somebody hung him in a closet overnight and he jumps out in the morning with his suit all bunched up and starts running around saying, 'I want to be president.'"

Bob Haldeman, Nixon's chief of staff, was especially in-flamed by what he saw as Ailes's treachery, and saw to it that there was no real job for him at the White House. From time to time he was summoned by the White House to undertake special assignments, such as producing Nixon's chat with Neil Armstrong during the moon landing, or helping with the media strategy after the crippled flight of Apollo 13—but he did these things pro bono. "I never even took a per diem, let alone payment," Ailes told me. "I didn't want to have to tell my kid someday that I had been on the government payroll." This may be sour grapes, but Ailes was indeed lucky that he didn't get drawn into the political side of the Nixon operation. "I was completely out of it in 1972," he says. "When the Watergate guys were going to jail, I was in Africa making a wildlife documentary with Bobby Kennedy Jr. Some people called me Houdini, but I was never even questioned. Not getting a job was the best thing that ever happened to me."

Looking back, Ailes has mixed emotions about Nixon. He admires his dogged persistence—his willingness to be the worst player on his college football team, a guy who got hammered every day at practice but kept coming back until he won a letter; and his insistence, as a candidate, on keeping every speaking commitment, no matter how trivial or logistically difficult (Nixon's insistence on going to Alaska on the last weekend before Election Day in 1960, while Kennedy campaigned in swing states, may have cost him the presidency). But he also sees Nixon's flaws, one of which was indulging in tough talk he didn't really mean. "Nixon thought that the 1960 election was stolen by the Daley machine in Chicago," Ailes told me, "and he had a lasting fear that the Kennedys would do it again in 1972. He believed the Democratic National Committee might be planning to replace George McGovern with Teddy. I wasn't at the White House but I heard that Nixon said that somebody should look into it. Nixon was always saying things like that, and people around him understood that he didn't necessarily mean them literally. But Gordon Liddy was there, and he may have taken it as a marching order. With a guy like that, who burns his fingers for fun, you have to be careful about what you say and how you say it."

In 1969, Ailes left Washington. "I drove up to Manhattan in an old Pontiac and hit a snowstorm where I got stuck for about ten hours," he recalls. "I got into town about 2:00 a.m. Next day I rented an apartment on Eighth Avenue." He started his own company, Ailes Production, later changed to Ailes Communications.

Marjorie stayed in Philadelphia. They weren't officially divorced for five more years, and they saw each other occasionally, but the marriage was over. "We just grew apart," Ailes says. "She was into art and literature, and she had a lot of local interests. I was after a national career, and I was selfish. We had no kids, and it ended amicably. We shared a divorce lawyer and parted as friends."

In the meantime, Ailes Communications was building quite a multifaceted operation. Over the years, Ailes produced commercial television documentaries as well as off-Broadway plays. He consulted for local television stations around the country. He even tried his hand at talent management. His best-known clients were Kelly Garrett, a beautiful actress with whom Ailes had a close personal relationship, and satirist Mort Sahl, whose career was in decline when Ailes picked him up. "Mort was still brilliant but he was unreliable," Ailes says. "One time he came to Buffalo for a gig and refused to leave the airport because the limo was the wrong color." That experience inspired Ailes to leave the talent management game.

Ailes Communications did a lot of corporate and commercial work for a list of clients that ranged from Polaroid and the Texas Energy Commission to the American Kennel Club. Ailes did issue ads for the American Bankers Association, consulted on messaging and positioning for Philip Morris, and provided executive training to American Express, General Electric, and others. His clients knew that he had Washington connections, which were bolstered by his growing reputation as a major factor in Republican politics.

"Roger Ailes was the first independent political consultant," says political consultant Dick Morris, now a commentator on Fox News. "Before him, candidates hired advertising agencies or executives to do their media, or turned it over to the party. Roger was the first guy to hang out his own shingle and take clients. It would be fair to say that he invented the modern profession of political consulting." This isn't strictly true: There have been professional campaign consultants going back at least to the early 1930s, when a pair of Californians, Clem Whitaker and Leone Baxter, founded Campaigns, Inc. But Ailes was among the first, and certainly the most successful, in the era of televised national politics. He was always a Republican, but from the start he approached his campaigns with a nonideological detachment. One of his early clients was Jim Holshouser Jr., a young attorney who, in 1972, was running to become the first Republican governor in the history of North Carolina. At the time, one of the hottest issues was school busing to achieve racial integration. It was extremely unpopular, not just in the South but in liberal bastions like Boston; in my hometown, Pontiac, a Democratic stronghold, crowds overturned and burned school buses. Holshouser's Democratic opponent was opposed to busing, so it didn't seem like a problem until the candidate told Ailes that it was. "We are going to support busing," he told his consultant.

"When a candidate begins saying 'we' it usually means that his wife is involved," says Ailes. Sure enough, Mrs. Holshouser turned out to be a staunch supporter of school busing, and she convinced her husband that he should be, too.

Ailes had a heart-to-heart with Holshouser. "I have no fucking idea if busing will work or not," he said. "I haven't seen any data on it, I don't know the issue. I don't know if it is a good thing, or a bad one. But here is what I *do* know. If you don't do an antibusing spot on TV, you will lose the election. Now, if I were you I'd do the fucking spot, win the election, and then, once you're in office, do whatever you think is right. Or, you can not do the fucking spot, make your wife feel better, and not be governor, in which case you won't be able to do anything about the issue one way or the other. But that's not my problem. I'm going to cash my check before Election Day and be back on a plane for New York before the votes are counted. You have to live here. It's your life and your decision."

I asked Ailes what happened.

"He did the spot and won."

"And what did he do about busing?"

Ailes seemed surprised by the question. "I have no idea," he said.

For the next decade, Ailes kept up a frenetic schedule. He produced Broadway shows, including *Mother Earth*, a short-lived environmental musical, as well as *The Hot l Baltimore*. He traveled to Africa to shoot a wildlife documentary starring Bobby Kennedy Jr. He and John Huddy (and, typically, two of Huddy's children now work for him) made a TV special on Federico Fellini, *Fellini: Wizards, Clowns and Honest Liars*. He consulted for local television stations around New York and the country, and he took on corporate clients as an expert in image making and damage control. He also made his first venture into conservative television. In 1973, Joseph Coors, a right-wing multimillionaire, sought to combat the ideological tilt of the networks by establishing his own TV news provider, Television News, Inc. (TVN). Ailes served as a consultant who had a license to fire, and he used it to get rid of some thirty employees. One he kept was Charlie Gibson, who went on to a distinguished network career. But no amount of hiring and firing could save TVN. Conservative television news was an idea whose time had not yet come. It closed in 1975 and Ailes busied himself with his filmmaking and his commercial and political clients.

In 1980, a Long Island machine politician named Al D'Amato came to see Ailes. He had unseated the venerable incumbent senator, liberal Republican Jacob Javits, in a nasty primary in which D'Amato illustrated Javits's old age and precarious health by showing a kid popping a balloon. Javits, who was in the early stages of Lou Gehrig's disease, responded by running against D'Amato in the general election on the Liberal Party ticket. The Democrats fielded Congresswoman Elizabeth Holtzman.

"I went from 'Al who?' to a nasty guy," says D'Amato. "People hated those ads and I don't blame them." He realized that he had no chance unless he could change his image in a hurry. He went to see Roger Ailes.

Ailes looked at the situation and came to a simple conclusion: D'Amato was perceived as a jerk. "Jesus, nobody likes you. Your own mother wouldn't vote for you. Do you even have a mother?" D'Amato assured him that he did, in fact, have one, and Ailes proceeded to turn her into a television star. In what became known as the "mama" ad, he showed an elderly woman, returning from the market with an armful of groceries, talking about how hard it was these days (of Carter-era inflation) for the middle class to make ends meet. Then she turned to the camera, introduced herself, and told viewers that if they wanted things to change they should vote for her son, Al D'Amato.

"That ad was stupendous," says D'Amato. "Everybody loved

her. [Liberal columnist] Jimmy Breslin wrote, 'I'd never vote for Al D'Amato, but I'd vote for his mother.' That one spot turned the election around, and made my victory possible." It was a narrow victory—he got fewer than half the votes in the three-way race—but a win is a win and he spent the next eighteen years in the Senate.

By 1998, Ailes was out of the consulting business and running Fox News, but he is not the kind of guy who loses touch with old friends and clients, and he agreed to meet with D'Amato for a friendly chat about the senator's political future. D'Amato wanted a fourth term. Ailes advised against it. "You've had three. What do you need another one for?" he asked. He told D'Amato he would probably lose, and he did, defeated by Representative Chuck Schumer. Without Ailes, D'Amato ran a tasteless campaign whose low point came when he called Schumer a putz-head. Today, he says he should have listened to Ailes. "The thing about Roger is, he doesn't tell you something he doesn't believe. If he tells you something, take it to the bank. But he tells you and that's that. He doesn't insist that you agree with him."

Ailes's early successes with D'Amato secured him a place as a New York Republican power broker. He became one of the de facto leaders of the GOP in the Empire State. Tim Carey, a longtime Republican operative, worked on New York campaigns for Javits, Ronald Reagan, Jack Kemp, and George Pataki, and served as a consultant to the Republican National Committee. Carey also worked for Lew Lehrman, the drugstore magnate who ran against Mario Cuomo in the 1982 New York gubernatorial race. "Lehrman was stiff," recalls Carey. "I took him to Roger to learn how to communicate." Lehrman improved, but not enough to defeat Cuomo, who didn't need lessons to connect with the public.

That same year, the job of Westchester county executive

became vacant. Tony Colavita, the outgoing incumbent, needed to pick a successor from a roster of aspiring candidates, including future governor George Pataki, who was then mayor of Peekskill. Colavita brought his potential successors down to Ailes Communications one at a time and Ailes checked them out, taping and assessing speeches. He settled on Andy O'Rourke of Yonkers. "Let's just say Andy was the kind of guy who would wear two different plaids," says Carey. "But Ailes saw past that. To him, O'Rourke was like a guy from *GQ*, a winner. And Roger was right about him—he was reelected three times and then went on to be a state judge." Pataki didn't get the job, but there were no hard feelings. "Roger thought he was too young," says Carey.

Carey worked with Ailes on numerous campaigns and came away with an education. "Roger taught me to always be honest with candidates, and firm. In political consulting you have a lot of clients who mistakenly think they know more than they do. And every candidate meets people who have ideas. Roger could say no. He fought for his candidates, but he didn't empathize with them."

"He also taught me that there is no cookie cutter. A lot of consultants work with a one-size-fits-all pattern, and they lose. But for Roger, it was always a matter of sizing up the opponent, finding his weaknesses, or turning his strengths against him."

For years, Ailes had lived a peripatetic single life. He met lots of women at shoots and on the trail and he dated from time to time, but he was more interested, he says, in work. But as time went on, he began to yearn for family life. In 1981, he married Norma Ferrer, a divorced mother of two, whom he met in Florida, where she worked at an ad agency at whose facilities Ailes was editing the documentary on Fellini. Ferrer had two children: a son, who was living on the West Coast with his father, and a daughter, Shawn. "I didn't adopt Shawn," Ailes says. "She called me Roger, not Dad, but I did everything for her that a dad would do and I stayed married to her mother until she was in college." Ailes and Norma were divorced after eleven years. After the divorce, Norma went to work for Mission Broadcasting, an evangelical television production company. Shawn majored in journalism at the University of Georgia, moved to New York, and is now an executive at HGTV.

■ ■ ■

Ailes sat out the seventies in presidential politics, but he was active in the 1980 Reagan-Carter contest as a member of the Tuesday Group, a weekly gathering of senior image makers.

He played a more dramatic role in 1984, when he was called in to coach Ronald Reagan in his second debate with Walter Mondale. It was emergency surgery. Reagan, who was seventy-four, had appeared old and befuddled in the first debate, misstating facts, wandering off topic, and reinforcing the Democratic charge that he was too old for the job. The Reagan inner circle, led by his wife, Nancy, blamed Reagan's debate coaches and handlers for failing to prepare her husband. They were especially angry at David Stockman, the young director of the White House Office of Management and Budget, who had been tapped to play Mondale in rehearsal debates and had gone after Reagan so hard that, at one point, while talking about Social Security, the president lost his customary geniality and shouted at Stockman to shut up. Nancy Reagan thought the mock debates had undermined her husband's confidence. So did the head debate coach, Richard Darman. Ailes was called in.

Reagan biographer Lou Cannon describes the intervention:

Ailes knew that Reagan needed praise, not criticism, and interrupted the first rehearsal of the [second] debate to declare that the president had just given a "terrific answer" to some minor question. . . . Ailes told the president not to bother with facts and figures but to concentrate on the big themes. And he frankly raised the subject everyone had been avoiding: Reagan's age. He told Reagan that the entire country was now wondering if he was past his prime. He needed a response to that. Reagan came up with a quip, which he used at the second debate: "I will not make age an issue of this campaign. I am not going to exploit, for political purposes, my opponent's youth and inexperience."

Even Mondale laughed, and the issue of Reagan's age disappeared. Ailes, who had learned from his McGinniss experience to stay in the background, did not take credit for the change. He didn't need to; everyone in Washington knew.

Ailes became a favorite of the Reagans, who grew comfortable enough with him to permit an occasional glimpse past their "Ronnie-Mommy" image. "We were taping an antidrug commercial," Ailes recalls. "It was probably the first time they had acted together since *Hellcats of the Navy* in 1945. Nancy kept giving the president line readings—'do this, do that'— stopping the teleprompter and the tape. I could see that the president was getting pissed off at her and finally he said, 'You know, I've actually done this before.' Nancy glared at him and marched out of the room. Reagan and I just stood there, looking at each other, and I was thinking, What the fuck happens now? The commercial was written for two people, and one of them was gone. I said, 'Mr. President, what are our plans?'

"Reagan didn't bat an eye. He said, 'Let's watch the football game. She'll be back in fifteen minutes.' I forget who was playing but we sat there and watched, and after fourteen minutes and fifty seconds, Nancy walked back into the room. She was chilly but professional—they were both actors when you come down to it, and we finished the shoot with no more problems. People say that Nancy ran him, and maybe sometimes she did, but I saw a different side of that relationship."

In 1989, Ailes published *You Are the Message*, a book that still earns royalties more than twenty years later. (This is rare—trust me.) A review on CNN called Ailes "one of the best debate coaches in America." In macho style, he began the book with a story about how he stared down and tamed Charles Manson during a prison interview.

You Are the Message was aimed primarily at corporate executives who wanted to improve their public performance, especially on television. The prescriptions have an unmistakable Fox News flavor. To be a really good communicator, Ailes wrote, "you have to be punchy and graphic in your conversation—at least some of the time—to hold people's interest."

He also offered advice to would-be politicos. "There are heart issues and head issues. You can talk about taxes and roads and those are head issues. They require intellectual conceptualization. But if you start talking about abortion, missing children, or health care, those are heart issues. They concern people."

Ailes has become increasingly disenchanted with the format of presidential debates, which he considers formulaic, predictable, and unenlightening. "I'd stage a series of three debates, so that if somebody screws up, there's a chance to fix it next time. I'd hold the debates in an empty studio, nobody there but the two candidates sitting face-to-face and five cameras. No audience. No questioners. No moderator. I wouldn't even tell them who goes first, just turn on the lights and let them talk to each other. That's the debate that I'd like to see."

■ ■ ■

Over the years, Ailes stayed in touch with his old boss, Woody Fraser, who was in New York producing network shows including *Good Morning America* and *Nightline*. They sometimes met for lunch at the Redeye Grill in Midtown, near Ailes Communications. "Roger was very proud of his company and the clients he had," says Fraser. "He had become a man of the world. I was impressed by the fact that he knew how to get things done without breaking legs or screaming, which were my usual methods as a producer."

One of Fraser's projects was a talk show hosted by basketball legend Bill Russell, an intimidating figure with a keen intellect and an ego to match. The show got off to a rocky start: Fraser couldn't get his star to take it seriously or prepare. "I'd go up to his apartment, which was always filled with friends and old teammates walking in and out, a real party scene. I'd try to sit him down and get him ready for the show. He was nice, but he didn't really pay much attention. I very much wanted this to work—I was a huge Russell fan—and I went to Roger for advice."

As Ailes diagnosed the problem, Fraser had himself to blame. Ailes told him, "Don't go up to his place; make him come to your office, no distractions. It will make him realize you are in charge, and that you mean business."

"I was pissed off," said Fraser, "but I took the advice. Russell began coming to me. And you know what? He started doing his job and the show worked. It seems like a simple thing, but I realized that Roger had learned over the years how to manage powerful people." Ailes had dealt with a lot of them in his career, from Mike Douglas and Bob Hope to Dick Nixon and Ronald Reagan. But he had never really been the top banana. George H. W. Bush gave him that chance.

CHAPTER FOUR

1988

George H. W. Bush was elected president of the United States against all political logic. "It wasn't a tide-of-history election," says Democratic consultant Paul Begala. "Republicans had been in for eight years and people were ready for change. And the only vice president who had ever succeeded his boss after eight years in office was Martin Van Buren. It was Roger Ailes who created the dominant issues in that campaign. He did it by defining Dukakis. The campaign was incredibly impressive, and it was mostly because of Ailes. He has an intuitive grasp of what Bill Clinton calls 'walking around people.'"

Ailes played many roles. Brit Hume, who covered the campaign for ABC News, remembers him as a spine stiffener for the sometimes indecisive Bush. When Democratic candidate Michael Dukakis began publicly complaining about the aggressive tone of the Republican ads, some in the Bush camp counseled toning them down. Ailes advised the candidate to double down and tell his opponent to quit whining. It was a tactic that worked; it cast Dukakis as a wimp who couldn't take criticism.

Ailes also acted as Bush's morale officer. The patrician vice president had a tendency to come off as stiff and distant; Ailes wanted to keep him loose. Early in the campaign, Republican opposition researchers discovered that Dukakis, as governor of Massachusetts, once vetoed a law that would have made it illegal for humans to have sex with animals. It had been tacked onto a piece of legislation that Dukakis opposed; his veto was no more than pro forma. But Ailes found a use for it. During the campaign he frequently mentioned it, facetiously, as an issue that could be deployed. At the first debate, Ailes saw an opportunity. Bush seemed tense and nervous. Just before he took the stage, Ailes took him aside and whispered, "If you get in trouble out there, just call him an animal fucker." Bush cracked up. To further lighten the mood, Ailes looked across the stage at Bob Squier, Dukakis's consultant, and motioned that the Democratic candidate's fly was open, causing a disconcerting moment on the Democratic side.

Mostly, though, Ailes was the man whose political ads set the tone of the campaign and kept Dukakis on the defensive. The Boston Harbor ad was one of those. Dukakis had a strong environmental record, especially contrasted with Bush's history as a Texas oilman, and it earned him the support of the major green groups. Ailes decided to take that advantage away. He produced a commercial showing garbage and debris floating in the water of Boston Harbor, along with a sign that read Radiation Hazard: No Swimming, and a narration: "As a candidate, Michael Dukakis called Boston Harbor an open sewer. As governor he had the opportunity to do something about it but chose not to. The Environmental Protection Agency called his lack of action the most expensive public policy mistake in the history of New England. Now Boston

Harbor, the dirtiest harbor in America, will cost residents $6 million to clean. And Michael Dukakis promises to do for America what he had done for Massachusetts."

"I could almost see Dukakis drowning in the polluted water," says Tim Carey.

It was Ailes's idea to cast Dukakis as weak on national defense. Dukakis aided and abetted the effort by dressing up in a flak jacket and an oversized helmet to take a photo-op ride in the turret of an M1 Abrams tank in testing grounds near Detroit. The idea was to make Dukakis look like a commander in chief. In fact, he came off as ridiculous, a little boy playing soldier. Ailes let the footage of the grinning Dukakis speak for itself. Nothing could have better emphasized the difference between Dukakis and Bush, a World War II combat pilot.

The most infamous ad of the campaign was actually two ads, both on the subject of a Massachusetts prison furlough granted to an incarcerated murderer. Willie Horton was serving a life sentence for robbing and killing a seventeen-year-old gas station attendant. The crime was especially grisly: The victim was stabbed nineteen times and dumped into a garbage can.

There were other states (and the federal government) that had similar prisoner furlough plans. But they did not grant furloughs to murderers. The Massachusetts legislature passed a law to prevent such leniency, but Governor Dukakis vetoed it. He made the case that in 99 percent of cases, the furloughed prisoners returned without incident. It was his bad luck that Willie Horton belonged to the 1 percent.

In 1986, after more than a decade behind bars, Horton was released for a weekend. He traveled to Maryland, where he seized an engaged couple, knifed and tied up the man, and then proceeded to rape his fiancée twice as he looked on. The crime was so egregious that a Maryland judge refused to extradite him to Massachusetts on the grounds that he might again be furloughed.

The issue of the lenient Massachusetts furlough policy was first raised by Al Gore in the 1988 primary campaign, although Gore didn't actually mention Horton by name. In the fall presidential campaign the National Security Political Action Committee began running a TV ad, which did mention Horton and displayed his picture. The NSPAC was supposedly an independent player, although it was clearly pro-Bush, and then run by Larry McCarthy, a former employee of Ailes Communications who had left the firm to work for Bob Dole in the primaries.

The NSPAC ad was denounced as racially incendiary by the Democrats, and was dropped. Shortly thereafter a Bush ad called "Revolving Door," produced by Ailes, began airing. "Revolving Door" also attacked the Massachusetts prison furlough program, but it didn't use a photo of Willie Horton. Ailes didn't want to be charged with exploiting racial fears, as the NSPAC had. "At one point Lee Atwater [the hyperaggressive Republican campaign manager] handed me a picture of Horton and I tore it up," Ailes says.

Still, the two ads became conflated in the mind of the media.

In 1990, the Ohio Democratic Party lodged a formal complaint with the Federal Election Commission, charging that the Bush campaign had coordinated with the National Security PAC, which would have been a violation of campaign finance laws. The FEC split 3–3, and the case was dismissed.

During the campaign, Ailes himself exacerbated the impression that the Bush campaign was connected to the NSPAC ad. A *Time* magazine profile at the time quoted him as saying that "the only question is whether we depict Willie Horton with a knife in his hand or without it." Ailes doesn't deny he said it to reporter David Beckwith. "We were supposed to be off the record. Beckwith and I were friends and I was just joking," he told me. "Hell, I had no idea I'd be running a network someday."

The controversy over the Horton ad had a predictable effect. The media picked it up and ran the ads over and over; the glowering mug shot of the black murderer-rapist became familiar to millions. Atwater bragged that "by the time we're finished, they're going to wonder if Willie Horton is Dukakis's running mate." At Harvard's quadrennial electoral postmortem at the end of 1988—a seminar that includes the major professionals in all the campaigns—the Willie Horton ads were still a hot topic. Bob Beckel, a Democratic consultant who had run Mondale's campaign four years earlier, conceded that Ailes might not have ordered the NSPAC ad, but noted that there had been "a lot of Republican money behind it." Ailes responded by pointing out that the Dukakis campaign had run a similar commercial, featuring a woman in a body bag who had been raped and murdered by a Hispanic man on federal penal parole. Susan Estrich, Dukakis's campaign manager, fired back that the Democratic ad had been simple retaliation. "You want to play to fear, you've got your ugly story of a black man raping a white woman. Well, we'll tell you an even uglier story," she said.

Ron Brown, who headed Jesse Jackson's primary campaign and later served as Bill Clinton's secretary of commerce, seconded Beckel's accusation. "You knew what was happening," he told Ailes. "Maybe you couldn't control everything, but nobody stepped up to the plate and said, 'This is divisive, it's dangerous, it's wrong.'"

"So you're saying because he was black we can't use the issue?" Ailes shot back. "Despite the fact that he was a murderer and a rapist, he should have been given special treatment because he was black?"

There were many disputes at Harvard, but very little doubt about Ailes's crucial contribution to the Bush victory. Susan Estrich admitted that the campaign had been lost because the Republicans had seized control of the message and because "we didn't have a Roger Ailes. I mean two things. First, a person of his talent, because it's clear it doesn't matter unless you have his talent. But second, and perhaps equally important, a person whose judgment and relationship with the candidate is such that he had his trust and respect." Ed Rollins, who had been the campaign manager in Reagan's reelection campaign, agreed. "As much money as we spent in 1984, nobody ever moved the entire course of the campaign," he told his fellow participants. "There's no presidential campaign in the age of television where one ad, or a series of ads, really made a difference. I mean, people will go back and argue that the Lyndon Johnson daisy-plucker ad made a difference. The truth is, that ad was run once on network television. In this particular campaign, Roger's ads worked. . . . We have now come of age in presidential campaigns, with tough, hard-hitting negative comments in the arena. They will be here from [now] on."

Much of the 1988 Harvard seminar was given over to a discussion of the flaws of the American electoral process. Ailes himself raised the issue, and offered a typically pragmatic analysis. "When I get hired by a candidate, my job is to help him get elected. I would like to change the system. I would like to spend all of my time on deep issues and talk about the homeless problem and figure out how to solve it, but it's damn hard to do it in a ten-week campaign when you are getting banged around by the opponent and the press is interested in pictures, mistakes, and attacks." Ailes said that no single consultant or campaign manager could effect change. "Unless we are all willing to admit that we have a stake in it, to admit that we had a part of it and discuss mistakes we've made, it ain't ever going to change, folks. It's going to get tougher. And next time it's going to be six-second sound bites."

There is etiquette among political professionals. Like defense lawyers and prosecutors, they accept the verdict and move on. Politics is business; personal animosity is for amateurs. Ailes has always set an example. In the eighties, the top Democratic consultant was Bob Squier. He and Ailes faced each other in a series of campaigns and, for five years, as debate partners on *The Today Show*. They would put each other down on the air and then go out to dinner afterward. When Squier died, Ailes wrote a glowing eulogy in *Time* magazine and spoke at his funeral.

Most of the pros at Harvard observed this rule. But one, Jack Corrigan, a senior Dukakis operative, insisted on refighting old battles. He accused Ailes of running a dirty campaign. "The difference between the two campaigns, and the way we [portrayed the two candidates] . . . is the difference between truth and fiction," he said.

"Oh, come on," said Ailes in a dismissive tone.

Corrigan was undeterred. "Michael Dukakis took very specific positions on all of the issues. Your candidate had fundamentally flip-flopped on basic values, in particular on the abortion question and on what he once called 'voodoo economics.'"

Ailes reminded Corrigan that Dukakis, too, had changed positions on trade and weapons systems.

"That's not true," snapped Corrigan. "The positions as you characterized them are not correct . . . he ran on his values. He had a firm set of beliefs."

"I don't believe that at all," said Ailes. "He ran to the right. He ran as a moderate. He didn't run as a liberal."

"You can't imagine a different worldview than your own," said Corrigan.

"Don't attack me personally. There's no need for that," Ailes said.

The exchange was an excellent illustration of why Ailes was so effective. Corrigan saw the election as a battle between virtue and sin. If an Ailes opponent insisted on believing in fairy tales about the virtuous Sir Michael and the evil George Bush, so much the better. Corrigan was making the cardinal mistake of campaign operatives. He believed his own bullshit. And he took it personally.

Ailes never did. In fact, he used the Harvard seminar to network with the enemy. You never know when a senior liberal might come in handy. Eventually he hired Susan Estrich and Bob Beckel as commentators at Fox. He also hired Geraldine Ferraro, a liberal New York Democrat who in 1984, as the first female vice presidential candidate, had been Beckel's candidate.

■ ■ ■

The 1988 election made Ailes into the first superstar political consultant, so famous and infamous that his mere participation in a campaign became an issue. George Voinovich wanted him enough to risk his own family.

Voinovich was the ex-mayor of Cleveland, acclaimed for bringing the city back from the racial and financial troubles that had typified it. In 1988, before the presidential election, he decided to run for the Senate against incumbent Howard Metzenbaum, and he wanted Roger Ailes on board. They were fellow graduates of Ohio University. Ailes knew Ohio politics, and Voinovich had never run statewide. But there was a problem.

"My brother was married to Mike Douglas's daughter," recalls Voinovich. "And Douglas was still teed off at Roger for leaving his show and going into politics. My brother heard I was going to hire Roger and he begged me not to. 'Mike won't be happy,' he said. I don't know if he asked him, but I didn't hire Roger." Nineteen eighty-eight was a Republican year in Ohio: George H. W. Bush won the state by 11 percent. But Voinovich lost to Metzenbaum by fourteen points. The campaign was amateurish and nasty (at one point Voinovich accused his opponent of being soft on child pornography) and it left him bruised but determined. Two years later, when he decided to run for governor, he informed his family that he was going to hire Roger Ailes whether Mike Douglas liked it or not, and he did.

"Why did I do it? I wanted Roger on my side. Going into the race I was behind my opponent in fund-raising by $3 million. Roger's reputation was so good among Republicans that the mere fact that he was with me made it possible to close the money gap. Roger Ailes gave me gravitas."

Ailes might have been popular with Republicans, but he was a target to Democrats. When he went to Columbus, a group of protesters passed out leaflets denouncing him; *Newsweek* reported that Ailes had made history by becoming "the first consultant on record to be the target of a demonstration."

Voinovich had already lost his first debate against Democratic candidate Anthony Celebrezze Jr. Celebrezze had been a vocal supporter of abortion choice, but when he flipped to pro-life in the debate, he caught Voinovich off guard. "When Roger came in, the first thing he did was tag Celebrezze on the character issue, as a man who believed one thing and said another," Voinovich says. Then, with Celebrezze on the defensive, Ailes concentrated on rebuilding his own candidate's morale.

"Roger gave me confidence going into the second debate. He told me, 'Don't worry, you know this stuff!' He took away my note cards. 'You don't need any cards to prompt you. Just be yourself.' It was the Holy Spirit and Roger who got me through that debate," he says.

Ailes also created ads that would humanize the reticent Voinovich. One, titled "Best Decision," showed the candidate frolicking with his family. "Roger told me, 'There are very few candidates who can twirl their wife around in a campaign ad. You can because it's obvious that the two of you love each other.' I said, 'Yes, but I never twirled my wife around a stage.' To which he replied, 'Doesn't matter, twirl her.'" Voinovich did. "That was one of the best ads I ever did," says Ailes today. "If Mitt Romney had done one like it in the primary campaign, it would have solved his lack-of-warmth issue."

"What Roger did for me was above and beyond what a consultant does for a client," says Voinovich. "He got into the fight. A lot of big-time consultants work hard and then they go out and play hard, but that's not Roger. He's not the kind of guy who went out and had a few drinks with the boys. He worked his butt off and cooled out after work, by himself. I have to say that I really admired him. I still do."

In Ohio, Ailes followed his custom of not involving himself much in his client's platform. "Roger didn't get involved with advocating any positions. He's ideological today, but he wasn't back then. What he did was make sure we knew what we were talking about. In 1988, my research was terrible. Roger made sure that didn't happen again. He could see down the road, and look at things five different ways. He never got surprised."

With Ailes at the helm, Voinovich won handily. And the story had a happy family ending. At a fund-raiser in Cleveland, Ailes and Douglas met, shook hands, and made up. Nobody was more relieved than Governor Voinovich's brother. Ailes was happy, too. He and Douglas had been close during their years on the show, their desks literally next to each other in the cramped office in Cleveland, and it hurt Ailes when Douglas's wife called him disloyal and Douglas predicted to the staff that Ailes would fail. "Later on he took credit for my success," says Ailes. On one of my visits to Fox, he showed me a clip of a television interview Douglas did in 2005, in which he called his former producer "brilliant" and "amazing. Somebody you want to listen to." Ailes smiled with satisfaction. "He never said anything like that when we were together."

Ailes loved winning in the Voinovich campaign in Ohio. He loved winning anyplace, and he often did. In more than 140 campaigns he orchestrated, he estimates that his victories outnumbered his losses by about nine to one. "A lot of consultants try to stick to races they can win, in which their candidate is a favorite," he says. "I didn't do that. I took and won some pretty outside shots, like Holshouser in North Carolina, or Mitch McConnell, a county executive in Kentucky up against an incumbent senator. Sometimes I won those, and sometimes I lost if the guy wasn't a good candidate. But with a good candidate and enough money, I didn't lose many. And I never lost a race where I felt outproduced or outmaneuvered."

Or outcompeted. "There was a consultant I was up against once in Baltimore," Ailes says. "He told a reporter that there are a lot of consultants who will kill for their candidate, but

Ailes is the only one ready to die for his." But it was an arrangement that ended when the campaign did.

Nobody wins all the time. In 1982, Ailes's candidate, Harrison Schmitt, lost a Senate race in New Mexico to Jeff Bingaman. His opponent in that contest was a young consultant named Dick Morris, whose star client was the governor of Arkansas, Bill Clinton. After the election, they went to lunch and Ailes told Morris that people considered him a brilliant young guy, but worried about his loyalty and character and wondered if he was a team player. Evidently Morris calmed those fears, because in 1988, Morris did consulting work for the Bush campaign. When the Lewinsky scandal broke, Ailes put Morris on the air as a Fox contributor. "Roger hired me because he wanted someone who had been in the Clinton White House and who knew how to interpret what was happening there," Morris says.

In 1989, Ailes signed on to run Rudy Giuliani's first campaign for mayor, against David Dinkins, who had defeated incumbent Ed Koch in the Democratic primary. Dinkins won the race by the narrowest margin in New York City history, and became the city's first (and so far, only) African American mayor. Ailes kept up his friendship with Giuliani. In 1996, then in office, Mayor Giuliani lobbied for Fox News to get carriage rights for New York City, a critical factor in the success of the network. Typically, Ailes also stayed on good terms with Dinkins.

■ ■ ■

By 1991, Ailes was getting tired of politics. He had been a political television producer, a debate coach, an ad maker, and a strategist for presidents. He had a client sitting in the Oval Office at the time, and lesser candidates standing in line for his services. He was, at fifty, an elder statesman and a mentor to consultants on both sides of the political aisle. "Roger invented the orchestra pit theory," says Bob Beckel. "Campaigns are just a series of moments that people remember. If you have two guys onstage and one guy says, 'I have a solution to the Middle East problem,' and the other guy falls in the orchestra pit, who do you think is going to be on the evening news?"

But Ailes had been in one too many orchestra pits. That year his candidate, Dick Thornburgh, the former U.S. attorney general, lost a Senate race in Pennsylvania to Harris Wofford, a relative unknown. Wofford's consultants were James Carville and Paul Begala. "I had followed Roger's career since I was a student at the University of Texas," Begala says. "To tell you the truth, I was thrilled to be up against him."

The feeling wasn't mutual. Ailes is on good terms with Carville, despite the fact that Carville recently blurbed an anti-Ailes book by David Brock, the head of the progressive watchdog group Media Matters for America. That, Ailes assumed, was just business. But, like Jack Corrigan, Begala insulted him personally. Worse, he did it publicly, in a joint appearance on ABC's *Nightline*. In the heat of battle, Begala called Ailes "a Madison Avenue blowhard." Ailes responded by inviting Begala to step outside. It was a symbolic invitation—they were in separate studios in different time zones—but the sentiment was real. But Begala, at least, has no hard feelings. "I have limitless professional respect for Roger Ailes," he told me.

Thornburgh was Ailes's last campaign. "I was coming back from Los Angeles on Christmas Eve on the red-eye," he recalls, "and I realized that everyone who worked for me was at home with their families. I was out there all alone and I was sick of it. By then I hated politics. And so I quit running candidates." Ailes met informally with George H. W. Bush during the 1992 race, "just to lighten him up a little," but his career as a full-time consultant was over. His mind was now on other things. He wanted to get back into his first love: TV.

CHAPTER FIVE

TELEVISION NEWS

Over the years, Ailes had always combined his political and corporate consulting with television production. In addition to his stint at TVN, he produced *Tomorrow with Tom Snyder*, NBC's precursor to *Late Night with David Letterman*; made some highly regarded documentaries that were sold to stations around the country; and did consulting work for local stations, including the *Washington Post*'s affiliates.

In 1991, Rush Limbaugh's radio show was a phenomenal success, the biggest thing on AM radio. One night Limbaugh was dining at one of his favorite New York restaurants, "21," when Roger Ailes walked over and introduced himself. "I was in awe of him," Limbaugh recalls. "I was amazed he even knew who I was. He said that his wife listened to me all day, every day."

Limbaugh and Ailes hit it off immediately. They had a great deal in common. Both were products of small-town midwestern America, shaped by the conservative values of the Eisenhower era and the sometimes harsh discipline of stern fathers. They had both been indifferent and rebellious students—Limbaugh dropped out of a second-rate college after one year—who made their bones as media showmen. And they were both more than willing to mix it up with the liberal establishment.

Ailes told Limbaugh that they should do a television show together. At first Limbaugh thought it was a bad idea—he had never hosted a television show before—but Ailes convinced him that it would work. "Rush said he didn't want guests on the show," Ailes recalls. "He said he didn't need them, because he didn't care what anybody else thinks. There were very few people, then or now, who could hold a television audience all alone on the screen or who even had the balls to try. The only model I had was Bishop Fulton J. Sheen's program, and I thought Rush could carry it off."

Ailes couldn't find a network that would carry the controversial Limbaugh's one-man show. He decided to resort to syndication, which had worked beautifully for Mike Douglas. He reached out to Woody Fraser, who took the idea to Bob Turner, who was the head of Multimedia Entertainment (and later became a Republican congressman from Manhattan).

Limbaugh's TV show was taped before an audience and ran five days a week for half an hour. Like the radio show, it consisted of Limbaugh riffing off the news. "Everybody marvels at Jon Stewart's show," says Limbaugh. "That's what my show was. That's what Roger and I did—find news clips and make fun of people who weren't used to being laughed at. We combined the comedy with dead serious political and cultural discussion."

Limbaugh believes that the TV show, which ran four years, provided a template for the Fox News evening format, although he concedes that Ailes probably doesn't agree. "Our premise of conservatism, unabashed and unafraid, was established once and for all on mainstream television. We showed it could be done," he says.

Ailes was Limbaugh's executive producer and he was also his mentor. Limbaugh, who was a decade younger and comparatively new on the national scene, leaned on his producer's sophistication in the ways of Washington and the New York media. When President George H. W. Bush invited them to the White House for a sleepover, it was Ailes who told him it was all right to call his mom from the Lincoln Bedroom.

The media were, of course, interested in the pajama party at 1600 Pennsylvania Avenue. Limbaugh cleared an invitation from *The Today Show* with Ailes, who gave him some media advice. "Roger told me that he had detected in me a common fault that newcomers to TV make when being interviewed by mainstream journalists. He said, 'Rush, they don't care what you think. Don't try to persuade them of anything. Don't try to change their mind. They are not asking you questions to learn anything. So don't look at this as an opportunity to enlighten them. Whatever they ask, just say whatever you want to say.'"

Ailes sometimes took a more direct approach in protecting his friend and star. They got wind that *Time* magazine was planning a cover story portraying Limbaugh and Howard Stern as similar figures. Ailes figured this would hurt the show and make it less attractive to potential advertisers. "Roger got in gear and called *Time* magazine. I sat in his office during the call," Limbaugh recalls. "He told them that if they persisted in this, we on the TV show would do features on all the reporters working on the story. That we would hire investigators to look into their backgrounds, find out how many DUIs they had, run a story demonstrating the similarities of these reporters to Al Goldstein [the publisher of *Screw* magazine]. It was a virtuoso performance. I was laughing my ass off. And I think it worked to an extent because when the story came out, it was basically harmless. That's the thing—when you have Roger Ailes on your side, you do not lose."

Limbaugh eventually left the show because he didn't like the meetings and collaboration that go with television, but he and Ailes have remained close friends, an alliance that has helped shape the tone and direction of the conservative movement and the Republican Party. Limbaugh—despite the fact that he is boycotting New York State because of what he regards as its confiscatory taxation policy—visits Ailes at his Putnam County mountaintop home from time to time; Ailes is a regular at Limbaugh's Palm Beach estate for the Spring Fling, a long weekend that brings Limbaugh cronies and political friends together for golf (which Ailes can't play), drinking (which Ailes no longer does), and conversations about the state of the world and the country. "Politically, Roger and I are brothers," Limbaugh says. "Trust me when I tell you there is never any strategy session, in the sense that we never coordinate content. There has never been a time where we even discussed mutual programming to achieve an objective. That never happens. It doesn't really have to. Ideologically and culturally, we are two peas in a pod."

While he was producing the Limbaugh show, Ailes began exploring a new frontier: cable news. CNN had gone on the air in 1980 to considerable derision: Ted Turner, its founder, was called crazy for imagining that a station based in Atlanta could make money providing around-the-clock news from all over the world to an initially small cable audience.

But Turner was right. Over time the cable audience grew and so did CNN's reach and reputation. During the 1991 Gulf War, it was the only American station with journalists in Baghdad, and its war coverage became the talk of the media world. Cable appeared to be the wave of the future, and the big networks wanted a piece of the action. NBC was especially keen to explore the new terrain. It already had a struggling business channel, CNBC, which it hoped to expand. NBC president Bob Wright saw that as just the beginning, and he reached out to Roger Ailes to run the channel. Jack Welch, the outspoken, politically conservative head of NBC's parent company, General Electric, blessed the decision. Both he and Wright had reason to be pleased by the results. When Ailes took over, CNBC's asset value was $400 million. When he left, two years later, it had more than doubled.

Ailes had been watching cable news from the sidelines, and he had an intuition that it should be personality-driven. He brought in Chet Collier, a Bostonian of the old school and thirteen years Ailes's senior. He had been Ailes's boss and mentor and drinking buddy at the Douglas show, and had promoted Ailes to the post of executive producer after Woody Fraser left. "Chet was a Kennedy liberal, but I didn't give a damn about his politics," says Ailes. "He was a brilliant television guy. And he could tell me the truth. A lot of times that's crucial, to have somebody around who isn't afraid. You need somebody with the kind of relationship that allows him to close the door and, one-on-one, tell the boss, 'What the fuck are you thinking?' Collier did that for me. If I did something he thought was wrong, he'd tell me straight out that I was full of shit."

Neil Cavuto was already at CNBC when Ailes arrived. "I was worried about how badly we were doing after five years on the air," he says, and the arrival of Roger Ailes, known then for his partisan political activities, didn't help much.

"Roger wasn't a GE executive type," Cavuto says. "Jack Welch went way outside the petri dish when he hired him. But when I met Roger I remember thinking, this guy has elected presidents—maybe he can help us."

Ailes began with research. He spoke to everyone at the network and grilled them about the most minute details of their jobs. Once he knew what was happening, he began to intervene. "He'd tell the graphics guy if the writing was too small," Cavuto recalls. "He'd call the sound guy and say that the volume was too low. Editorial meetings were opened up, and everybody, even production assistants or other junior staff, were encouraged to speak up. On the other hand, he made it clear that he was not going to put up with eye-rolling or negativity."

"When I got to CNBC, I found chaos and a lack of leadership," Ailes told me. "There were executives there who spent their days playing basketball or at the track. First thing, I told people to get their feet off the goddamn desk and get to work."

"Roger tested people," says Cavuto. "He called me in and said, 'People tell me you are cocky and arrogant and you constantly interrupt—' At which point I interrupted him and said, 'You're right but I'm working on it.'" Ailes laughed and said that he liked Cavuto's work. They have been together ever since.

He demanded that producers and reporters rethink their approach to business news. At the time, it was considered bad form for journalists to talk about ratings or network profits. "Our thought was, is this story important, not who will watch it," says Cavuto. Roger forced people to get out of the ivory tower. "Everything is financial in some way," he said. "You can make a story out of anything."

Ailes insisted on not insulting the audience. He informed his staff that he didn't want an antibusiness climate on a business network, or a lot of financial jargon. "Roger is a guy from the middle of Ohio, and he knows how people think," says Cavuto. Reporters who acted superior to the corporate leaders they interviewed or conveyed the message that capitalism was selfish and crass didn't find the Ailes's regime congenial.

But, in general, Ailes was popular with the troops. His television expertise and down-to-earth sensibility were welcomed. He knew everybody's name, learned their personal stories, and came to be known as a soft touch. He also mocked the fashionably healthy cuisine of the network's cafeteria, paying the cooks extra to prepare burgers and fries.

Ailes's style of wisecracking profanity contributed to his common touch. It also sometimes got him in trouble, especially when he let loose in public. He mocked Tom Rogers, who was president of NBC cable operations, as a "publicity seeker." He went on the *Imus in the Morning* radio show and speculated that President Clinton's schedule in New York might include a date with Olympic ice-skating champion Nancy Kerrigan. He made an ugly joke implying that Hillary Clinton might have had something to do with the fate of three administration lawyers—Webster Hubbell, Bernard Nussbaum, and Vince Foster—who were, respectively, under investigation, forced to resign, and dead. "I wouldn't stand too close to her," he said. These cracks were way out of character for an NBC suit, which was just the way Ailes wanted it. Complaints to the corporate office were brushed aside; he was making NBC too much money to be disciplined.

■ ■ ■

On the Fourth of July, 1994, CNBC launched a second network, America's Talking, the forerunner of MSNBC. He branded the overall product "First in Business, First in Talk" and hired compelling personalities, including liberals like Chris Matthews (former aide to Democratic Speaker of the House Tip O'Neill), Tim Russert (who had been an aide to New York Democratic senator Pat Moynihan), and Geraldo Rivera.

Ailes also hired a host for his morning show. Steve Doocy was an aw-shucks country boy from Clay County, Kansas, who had been working for various network affiliates for a decade. He sent a reel to Chet Collier, who invited him to the cable network's headquarters in Fort Lee, New Jersey, for a meeting.

"What do we need to know about you?" Collier asked Doocy.

"I like to sit in a baby pool filled with lime-green Jell-O with no pants on," he replied.

"Roger looked at me, grinned, and said, 'You're hired,'" Doocy recalls. Beth Tilson, the programmer in charge of the network (and years later Ailes's wife), signed off on the line.

The roster of America's Talking was composed of a seemingly random selection of programs. There was a daily talent show; a medical advice program; a review of new gadgets and technology; a newscast featuring positive stories called *Have a Heart*; a mental health call-in show, *Am I Nuts?*; an ongoing investigative series on government waste; and *AT In-Depth*, two hours of news and chat cohosted by Matthews. Ailes himself did an interview show, *Straight Forward*, in which he talked to guests, many of whom were showbiz friends like Broadway star Carol Channing or interesting counterculture figures such as Joan Baez. As an interviewer Ailes was cordial and easygoing, with a style resembling that of his old friend Brian Lamb, the founder of C-SPAN. Ailes had piled up a lot of on-air experience in his *Today Show* appearances with Bob Squier between 1989 and 1992, and he had often been a guest on other shows, but he wasn't especially interested in performing. He did it for the team. It was hard to lure top guests all the way out to Fort Lee to appear on a new cable channel. "I had a pretty good Rolodex," he says.

The electronic media landscape of the 1990s was marked

by an effort to understand and capture the technological opportunities offered by satellite, cable, and the Internet. Synergy was the order of the day. Time Warner acquired CNN and then merged with AOL, a combination that really worked. Roone Arledge, the head of ABC News, announced that he was getting into the cable news business, although nothing came of it. Meanwhile, NBC struck a deal with Microsoft for a new cable network, MSNBC, that would replace America's Talking and current affairs talk shows on CNBC. Bob Wright and the other corporate heads at 30 Rock didn't see a place for Ailes in this new alignment. He was too brash and too partisan for their new partner, Bill Gates. With oceans of Silicon Valley dollars swimming before their eyes, they were free to toss Ailes overboard.

"Roger was disappointed as hell that we sold America's Talking," Jack Welch says. "But he had built up a lot of animosity. People were jealous of his accomplishments."

Wright appointed Andrew Lack, the head of NBC News, to take over the new network. Lack was a charismatic former advertising executive who had turned NBC News around after a scandal. *Dateline*, a prime-time magazine show, had faked an explosion of a GM truck in what turned out to be a bogus exposé.

It fell to Lack to clean up the debris. He was a big man with a bigger ego, who famously bragged to the *New York Times*, in 1997, that he was "America's news leader." NBC was content to let Ailes stay on at the helm of the new channel, but there was no chance that Roger Ailes was going to report to a man like Andy Lack. Ailes left Fort Lee, but he wasn't homeless. Rupert Murdoch was waiting for him on the other side of the Hudson.

Murdoch, whose trajectory had taken him from his native

Australia to London and then to the United States, already owned a string of broadcast stations, but wanted to go into the cable news business. He had an intuition that a large portion of the public was unhappy with the tone of mainstream TV news and would respond to a more patriotic, socially conservative, and less parochial sort of information. He and Ailes had met only once, briefly, on the Twentieth Century Fox movie lot years before, but they knew each other by reputation. "Roger had great success at CNBC and I heard that he was unhappy there," Murdoch says. "I asked him to come see me."

Ailes listened silently as Murdoch laid out his idea. "The question," Murdoch said, "is whether it can be done."

Ailes said that it could, but only if it could get on the air within six months, to beat MSNBC (and perhaps also ABC's new cable venture) to the punch. Ailes would be working from scratch. There were no studios, no equipment, no staff, and no infrastructure. Essentially he would be creating a network from nothing.

"How much will it cost me?" Murdoch asked.

"Nine hundred million to a billion," Ailes responded. "And you could lose it all."

"Can you do it?" Murdoch asked.

"Yes," said Ailes.

"Then go ahead and do it."

"I thought, either this man is crazy or he has the biggest set of balls I've ever seen," Murdoch says. Ailes was thinking pretty much the same thing about his new boss. Their negotiation was easy. "It was a fair deal," says Murdoch. "I'm a softie." In any case, Ailes wasn't in it primarily for the money. He was being given an opportunity to stick it to his critics at NBC, and to create something entirely new—a news network shaped in his image. Murdoch was only putting up a billion dollars; Ailes's reputation was at stake.

When news of the experiment got out, media sophisticates laughed as they had, fifteen years earlier, at Ted Turner. The *New York Times* was especially skeptical. "With no name and no formal plan for distribution, the promised channel inspired widespread doubts about its long-term survival among competitors and cable industry analysts. . . . The idea, some suggested, was to give Mr. Ailes a toy to play with, though given the current state of Fox News as described by some insiders, it may be less a toy than an imaginary friend."

But Jack Welch, watching from his suite at General Electric headquarters, knew this was no game. "I told them they would rue the day they let Roger team up with Rupert," he says. "You put a creative genius together with a guy with the guts and wallet of Rupert Murdoch and you have an unbeatable combination."

CHAPTER SIX

LINEUP

When Roger Ailes left CNBC, he was followed by more than eighty staffers in what is known in the lore of Fox News as "the jailbreak." These executives, producers, and on-air personalities became the backbone of the new network, and a large number are still there today. To this group, Ailes added close to a thousand staffers recruited from the ranks of television unknowns, underappreciated network personnel, or complete amateurs who had potential. His criterion was always the same. "In television, technology changes," he says. "The one constant is content. There has to be a show. And that's what I focused on—talent that could provide a show."

Ailes says he never did market research or focus groups. "I start with one question: Do I like the person? Of course, I also want to know how smart they are, if they can write and report, but it begins with a personal feeling. I was looking for people who could attract an audience. People who cared about who was watching. Getting ratings is how you get paid."

Chet Collier came over from CNBC to Fox as Ailes's chief lieutenant. And Ailes made an important acquisition in John Moody, a Cornell graduate with impeccable print credentials as UPI bureau chief in the former Soviet Union and France, and a decade as a senior *Time* magazine correspondent in Eastern Europe, Latin America, and the United States. Back in New York, a political and cultural conservative, Moody felt out of place. "I didn't enjoy the corridors of *Time*," he says. In 1996, public relations executive Howard Rubenstein told him that Rupert Murdoch and Roger Ailes were starting a news network. He was interested but also hesitant about joining a new venture.

"I was forty-three years old with a mortgage, a wife, and a dog," he says. Still, he went to a breakfast meeting in Ailes's office. "There was dust everywhere and exposed wires. We sat at a low table and Roger gave me terrible coffee and a bad bagel and we talked. There was a definite intellectual spark."

Their second meeting took place at a Chinese restaurant. Moody prepared by discussing the new venture with a friendly monsignor, who told him that everything happens for a reason. Ailes came prepared, too. "He took out a story I had written, pointed to something, and asked, 'What did you mean by this? Are you a liberal?'" Moody countered by mentioning that Ailes had produced Broadway shows with progressive themes. "I reminded him that there's a line in *The Hot l Baltimore* where a character says, 'We don't know how to dance but we must carry on as if we do.' Roger was impressed that I had done research on him before our meeting." Moody was hired as senior vice president for news.

Many of Moody's journalist friends disapproved. "Some of them thought I was being brought in to make the paint look new," he says. Others thought that Ailes, who had no real journalistic experience, lacked credentials. He was unmoved by this argument. "You don't need a license to do journalism," Moody says.

Moody's new job made him, in essence, the managing editor of the network, and he was soon accused by liberal critics of collaborating with Ailes and Murdoch in shaping a right-wing version of the news. The instrument of this control was allegedly a daily memo issued by Moody to reporters and producers. Moody saw this as nothing more than standard practice. "Networks all have directors, producers, reporters, and anchors," he says. "If each one did what he or she thought was best, there would be chaos. That's why news organizations all work from a plan, a starting point. That's why they are called organizations."

The daily memo became controversial after it was revealed in the documentary film *Outfoxed*, which was produced in 2004 by anti-Fox activist Robert Greenwald. In response, Ailes offered to publish 100 percent of Fox News' editorial directions and internal memos if competing cable news channels and broadcast network news divisions would do the same. So far, there have been no takers.

With Moody and Collier in place, Ailes went about building a lineup that would be able to compete with CNN and MSNBC. He needed a lead-off man, somebody genial and light enough to match the tone of the other morning shows, but with a sufficient edge to signal that Fox News was different. At CNBC, he had had Steve Doocy, but Doocy had left Ailes to host a morning comedy show on CBS's New York affiliate. The show wasn't funny and it was canceled within a month, leaving Doocy looking for work. He called Ailes, who told him that he had just one job left at Fox News—weatherman.

"I only did the weather once, in college," says Doocy. Ailes was unfazed by this. "Just keep it simple," he said. "All the squiggles are too complicated anyway. Just show me the high temperature and the low temperature and where it's raining. You try to sound like a genius, you baffle viewers. Don't get lost in the weeds." When Ailes started *Fox & Friends*, he made Doocy a permanent cohost (his current partners are Gretchen Carlson and Brian Kilmeade).

Fox & Friends is an easygoing program that delivers some hard political messages in the morning. Apart from Sean Hannity's show, it is probably the most blatantly partisan program on Fox. "We are who we are," Doocy says, as if they were an accidental conglomeration of talent. "You have a couple of kids and a mortgage; everyone winds up a little more conservative. All three of us are to the right, but we balance it with guests."

Fox & Friends does sometimes host liberal politicians. But since these politicians get asked tough and sometimes loaded questions, it is debatable whether they add balance or simply serve as targets.

When Doocy asked Howard Dean about reports that he had suffered a panic attack upon learning that as lieutenant governor of Vermont, he would be replacing the deceased incumbent, Dean indignantly denied it. Some exchanges with the opposition have been more congenial. When Tom Daschle was the Democratic majority leader of the Senate, he appeared on the show and did the weather. So did Henry Kissinger, an Ailes friend, to whom Doocy awarded a *Fox & Friends* "soap-on-a-rope" to go with his Nobel Peace Prize.

Shep Smith, one of the network's star news anchors, is another Fox original. He studied journalism at the University of Mississippi, failed to graduate, and spent a dozen years kicking around small stations in Florida and at the syndicated TV newsmagazine *A Current Affair*. He was in Los Angeles when he got a job offer from Ailes. The Fox chief was looking for

talent, but he was on a budget. "Will your agent act reason-
ably?" Ailes asked. Smith assured him that his agent was the
soul of reason. It was a good decision for both sides. In 2007,
the *New York Times* reported that Smith was making between
$7 million and $8 million—broadcast anchor money. "Roger
is fair. You go in to negotiate with him and there are certain
things he won't agree to, and if he says no, it's no. You don't
come back on that. And he's big on not letting people usurp
power. But the perks—vacation days, cars, assistants—all
those things are in the contract." What Ailes demands in return is that you do your job—and that you don't lie to him.

Ailes wanted Smith because of his informality. "I came up
in the era when the newscaster told you what was happening
and what to think about it," Ailes told me. "Fox changed that
some. It's very important to get the anchors on an even field
with the audience. Never let your talent talk down to people."

A lot of people at Fox think of Smith as a liberal, partly because he tends to wear his heart on his sleeve, especially on
issues with a racial component. A good ol' boy from Holly
Springs, Mississippi, who attended private segregated academies, he is, like a lot of Southerners of his generation, sensi-
tive to the legacy of Jim Crow and slavery. In his coverage of
Hurricane Katrina, he was visibly infuriated by the failures of
government, including the Bush administration, to relieve the
suffering of the victims. "When I got down there and saw
what was happening, I got in touch with Roger and he said,
'Bring in the cavalry. The government is lying? Get the word
out!' You don't expect people in the United States to be living
in third-world conditions."

Another crucial time in the cable day is 4:00 p.m., when
the markets close. Ailes gave the job to Neil Cavuto, one of
the original CNBC jailbreakers.

"I left money on the table when I came to Fox," Cavuto

says. "A lot of us did. This is an easy place to come to these days; we're like the Yankees in a good season. We pay better than the competition. But back then we didn't. Many, many of the people who left to go with Roger took pay cuts. Nobody's sorry."

Shortly after making the move, Cavuto was diagnosed with multiple sclerosis. He was fearful about breaking the news to his boss. "A lot of television executives would have wanted to get rid of me," he says.

Ailes asked how the disease might affect Cavuto's performance.

"It could cause me to lose my train of thought on the air," Cavuto said.

"Hell, you already do that," said Ailes.

"And I could lose the use of my legs."

"So what? If you do, we'll build you a ramp."

Cavuto is now in his sixteenth year in the 4:00 p.m. slot, and he is senior vice president of Fox Business Network. "I feel toward Roger like I do toward my own father," he told me. "He's somebody I can always count on."

This is a very widespread sentiment at Fox News, but it comes with a price. In Ailes's world, loyalty is rewarded, disloyalty punished. It is a point he made early, and emphatically, in the case of another financial journalist, Jim Cramer.

Cramer was a hot commodity when Ailes and Murdoch lured him to Fox News in 1999. A onetime president of the *Harvard Crimson*, he was a successful hedge fund manager and a well-known writer and commentator who appeared as a talking head on various network shows, including ABC's *Good Morning America* and CNBC's *Squawk Box*.

Cramer saw right away that Ailes could teach him how to be effective on television. "Life with Roger was an education," he says. "I learned more about TV from him than anyone else.

He invented the lightning round. He taught me that the only guests worth having on a business show are CEOs—take anybody lesser and it lowers your credibility. And he showed me the power of repetition. I once told him that I had said on the air three times how much I liked Apple stock. He laughed and said, 'Jim, after eighteen times, and only after eighteen times, will some Americans have heard it.'"

Another lesson was on the importance of longevity. "We were at a broadcast dinner and Ailes said, 'I'm going to introduce you to the most influential TV personalities in the room.' He took me over to meet Gene Rayburn, the game show host who had been on the air forever. 'People like him, they want him in their homes,' Roger said. He knew politics but these old show-business people, like Rayburn and Bob Hope and Judy Garland, were his real heroes."

A few years earlier, in 1996, Cramer and some partners started TheStreet.com, an early venture into financial cyberjournalism. Cramer joined Fox (and worked without monetary compensation) in order to leverage the exposure he would get for his website. Ailes thought having Cramer would draw viewers to the new channel. It was a classic nineties example of the theory and practice of synergy.

"I told Roger when he hired me that I'm a lifelong Democrat. I've given the party a lot of money over the years. Roger was joyous. 'Give more,' he said. 'I've got myself a real liberal.' I always expected there would be a catch, but there wasn't one."

Cramer's problem with Ailes wasn't political, it was personal. Cramer is hypercompetitive, but he couldn't match his boss's even fiercer dedication to winning, or the burdens it placed on him.

"Roger believes that you need to win every hour in order to win the next hour. Ratings at nine depend on ratings at eight.

And that's a team effort. Let's say you had a special coming up in the morning. The night before, you had to go on the prime-time shows in the last two minutes and hype it. You'd be on at 7:58, 8:58, 9:58, talk about what each host wanted to discuss and then at the end they say, 'So Jim, I hear you've got a show coming up tomorrow on greedy bankers. Give us an advance peek.' I'd say a few words about it and the host would go, 'Wow! Tune in tomorrow for that,' like they were enthralled. It wasn't a true shill exactly, but it's a way to build numbers."

Many years before, Marjorie Ailes had gone to Roger's boss at the Douglas show to complain about the hours. Now it was Karen Cramer's turn to get indignant. "She was just pissed off at how much time I spent away from home. The pressure built up and I talked to Roger, but his attitude was, 'This is the job, do it or not.'"

Cramer was under pressure from his investors to appear less on TV. They wanted him to give their money his full attention. His associates at TheStreet.com had different ideas about how he should spend his time. The cross-promotion they had envisioned at Fox wasn't working well. Kevin English, the site's CEO, convinced Cramer to hold a secret meeting with executives at CBS's financial show, *Market Watch*. Ailes, who is exceptionally well informed about matters that concern him, found out about it and called Cramer in. Cramer describes the experience in his autobiography, *Confessions of a Street Addict*. "[It was] one of those meetings where he would stare at you with those tungsten eyes of his, the same eyes that had stared down everyone from Nixon to Manson. I knew he knew." Ailes coldly reminded Cramer that they had a contract, and Cramer dropped the CBS initiative. But there was bad blood. A couple of months later, he was caught backstage on a hot microphone bad-mouthing Ailes. He apologized, but he knew he had crossed a red line. Soon after, he blew off a scheduled taping session. The final straw was mentioning his own stock as a buy on his show. By now, Cramer's marriage was falling apart, and he was being medicated for anxiety, but Ailes was unsympathetic. "Roger just said that we have a contract, and that's it. He fired me. We had worked together for two years but the truth is, he was right to fire me. And, despite everything, I still like him. He delivered on what he promised. I just wish, in retrospect, that I had, too."

The story of Cramer became a cautionary tale at the new network. Certain things were fine. You didn't have to be a Republican or a conservative. You could get away with coupling your commercial interests with your work as a commentator. You were welcome to be as eccentric as you liked. What you couldn't do was flout the rules, which Ailes set out in the employees' handbook and gave (and still gives) to new employees.

1. Excellence requires hard work, clear thinking, and the application of your unique talent. A desire to get better at your job every day is the cornerstone of a great career.

2. Nothing is more important than giving your word and keeping it. Don't blame others for your mistakes. Don't take credit for someone else's work. Don't lie, cheat, steal—people always figure it out, and you will never regain your reputation.

3. Our common goal is the success of Fox News. Only teams go to the Super Bowl. Volunteer to help others once your own job is finished. Ask for help when you need it. Solve problems together and give credit to others.

4. Attitude is everything. You live in your own mind. If you believe you're a victim, you're a victim. If you believe you'll succeed—you will. Negative people make positive

people sick. Management relies on positive people for all progress.

Cramer was a star, and a friend. But he hadn't been willing to work hard enough for the good of the team. He didn't keep his word. He had been publicly negative about his job and disrespectful to his boss. And so he was out. Ailes made an example of Jim Cramer; he wanted everyone to know that his handbook was not a set of lofty aspirations, but a guide to survival in Roger World.

Anchorman Mike Schneider didn't get it. He was a prototypical Fox hire, an experienced and competent newsman who had been at all three major networks but never quite reached the top. Ailes gave him a chance as host of a prime-time news show. It was a potential star-making job, but Schneider blew it.

In 1997, Fox TV broadcast the Super Bowl, including a halftime show by the Blues Brothers. This was a very big deal for the Murdoch-owned network, and as a cross-promotion for the fledgling Fox News, Ailes decided on a gimmick. At the end of the first half, Fox News anchor Catherine Crier broke in with a special news flash—the Blues Brothers had escaped from jail and were seen heading for the game. It got some media attention, which was Ailes's goal, but it offended Schneider's sense of propriety. He blasted the stunt in public. Ailes called him in and read him the riot act. "How dare you criticize your colleagues?" he said. "If I were in a foxhole with you, I'd shoot you first." Schneider's prime-time career was over, and Fox declined to renew his contract. After leaving the network, he ran for Congress in New Jersey as a reform Democrat, and lost.

The last case of blatant insubordination was the Paula Zahn affair. Zahn was a talented and glamorous CBS personality who came to Fox in 1999, anchored the nightly news, and then got her own show, *The Edge*, making her one of the first female prime-time hosts in cable news history. Less than two years later, Ailes discovered that although she was still under contract, she had been negotiating with CNN. This wasn't illegal, but it violated Ailes's sense of loyalty. The network sued Zahn, and while the case was thrown out, it made the point to all other employees that those who cross Roger Ailes won't be allowed to go quietly. Zahn went to CNN and then on to PBS, where she hosts cultural programs. Ailes eventually retaliated against CNN by poaching veteran journalist Greta Van Susteren and giving her a prime-time show of her own.

■ ■ ■

"In fifteen years, CNN and MSNBC have made sixty-three changes to their prime-time lineups," says Roger Ailes. "We've made five." Three anchors—Crier, Zahn, and Schneider—were replaced early on. In 2009, Alan Colmes was dropped from *Hannity & Colmes* (although he remains at Fox as a commentator). And famously, Ailes moved Bill O'Reilly from six o'clock to eight, setting off the most successful career in the history of cable news.

O'Reilly's office is on the seventeenth floor of the News Corp building. I was scheduled to meet him at five o'clock, but I arrived a few minutes early and ducked into the men's room. There I found O'Reilly staring at himself in the mirror as he brushed his teeth.

He looked at me backward and said, "Hi, Zev."

"How do you know it's me?" I asked.

"It's my job to know everything," he said, and invited me to continue the meeting in his office down the hall.

You don't just wander around Fox News randomly interviewing personnel. In every meeting there is someone, usually a member of the public relations staff, sitting in unobtrusively. O'Reilly had his own witness, Dave Tabacoff, the executive producer of his show, *The O'Reilly Factor*, who came over to Fox from ABC News. O'Reilly also placed a tape recorder prominently on his desk. The congenial mood of our bathroom encounter was replaced by a confrontational aura. Bill O'Reilly is not a trusting man.

But he trusts his boss. "There are very few honest television executives," he told me. "You can count them on the fingers of one hand." He raised a giant paw to demonstrate how few that actually is.

"When I was at CBS News, I covered the Falklands War," he said. "I was in Buenos Aires for the [Argentinian] surrender. When I got back to my hotel, my story was bigfooted by a CBS correspondent [he didn't say who, but he was referring to Bob Schieffer], a guy who had been afraid to go outside. He took my video, put his stand-up on it, and sent it."

O'Reilly was incensed. "I flew up to New York and said, 'What the fuck is this?' Their attitude was, 'Shut up, you're lucky to be at CBS.' So I left, and I was branded as a guy who isn't a team player. When ABC hired me I told Roone Arledge, 'Just don't bigfoot me,' and he didn't. But what happened at CBS was something that Roger Ailes would never allow. *Ever*."

O'Reilly knew Ailes from CNBC, where he sometimes sat in for Ailes on *Straight Forward*. On one such occasion he did an unusually tough interview of the New York Mets star Keith Hernandez, who had been caught using cocaine. "Why destroy your career?" he demanded.

"Afterward Roger told me that if he let me keep substituting for him, he wouldn't be able to book any guests," said O'Reilly with a grin.

O'Reilly bounced around ABC News and then, in 1989,

joined the staff of *Inside Edition,* becoming an anchor shortly after arriving. He was there for six years, won awards for his work, and left the show to enroll at Harvard's Kennedy School of Government, where he earned a master's degree in public administration. One of his teachers was former network newsman Marvin Kalb.

"Bill was an excellent student," Kalb says. "But I always had a feeling that no matter what I said or what he read, nothing changed his mind."

At Harvard, O'Reilly began plotting a return to television. Roger Ailes was just getting set up at Fox, and O'Reilly got in touch. "I told Roger that I had a written outline of a show I wanted to do," he says. "Roger told me, 'I don't need an outline. I know what you can do.'" Ailes was not impressed by O'Reilly's stint at Harvard, which he dismissively calls a "seven-week degree"; what he saw was O'Reilly's talent.

The show, originally called *The O'Reilly Report,* debuted at 6:00 p.m. Fox was available in about fifteen million homes at the time. "That's not even being on the air," says O'Reilly. But as the network's viewership expanded, Ailes decided to move O'Reilly's show to 8:00 p.m., where it took off. "In retrospect, it gave me a year to hone the concept," says O'Reilly. "And moving it to eight was smart. It meant that more young viewers could watch. A lot of television executives wouldn't have seen that. They don't even know the difference between six o'clock and eight."

The Factor has been the most watched prime-time show for more than ten years. Most nights O'Reilly's audience is larger than those of the shows on MSNBC, CNN, and CNBC *combined.* "I write the scripts myself, early in the day," he says. "I send them to Roger so he can see who I am interviewing and how I am framing subjects. But I have one hundred percent autonomy, and the system works perfectly."

O'Reilly and Ailes have had relatively few arguments over the years, but Ailes has made it clear to him that *he* runs the network and makes the final decisions.

O'Reilly's abrasive personality and amazing ratings have made him a target. He harbors a special animosity toward Jeff Zucker, the former head of NBCUniversal, whom he calls, with typical understatement, "the lowest form of humanity."

"Zucker decided to use MSNBC as a weapon to attack people and hired guttersnipes to do it. There were no boundaries; they launched personal attacks every night. How can you respect a news executive who allows that to happen?" At O'Reilly's behest, Ailes called Zucker and asked him to call off the anti-O'Reilly campaign, which was being led by Keith Olbermann. "Roger told him that he was putting people in jeopardy." When Zucker failed to respond, O'Reilly asked for, and got, protection. "You have a right to defend yourself," he says. "Roger gives me security. We're taking names. It's vicious, not something you just ignore."

There is widespread criticism of his relentless promotion of his bestselling books and public appearances. "He says he gives a lot of the money to charity and maybe he does," a senior executive at the network told me. "But he does it for free on Murdoch's air, so maybe Murdoch deserves some of the credit."

O'Reilly is not a candidate for colleague of the year at Fox. O'Reilly and Sean Hannity don't speak, and he doesn't "hand off" his program to Hannity at 9:00 p.m. with an introductory phrase, as is customary. He attributes this to technical difficulties, although it is a problem other anchors seem to have solved. Hannity, for his part, praises O'Reilly's talent and contribution to Fox, but concedes that he and his fellow Fox star don't talk to each other—quite a feat considering that the two men work on the same floor, within a hundred feet of each other's offices.

Hannity is a star in his own right, the Scottie Pippen to O'Reilly's Michael Jordan. His show is the second-most-watched prime-time cable news program; it, too, often beats the combined opposition. Like O'Reilly, Hannity grew up in an Irish Catholic family on Long Island and, as has become de rigueur at Ailes's network, he flaunts his working-class credentials. As a kid he scrubbed pots and pans in a restaurant kitchen, worked on construction projects, and did poorly at the preparatory seminary he attended.

O'Reilly developed his TV chops over a long career. Hannity is an Ailes creation. He was an AM talk show host in Atlanta when he applied for a job at Fox. What he brought to the table were boyish good looks, a nice clear tenor voice, a simple conservative perspective, and an important friendship with Newt Gingrich, the Georgia congressman who led the 1994 GOP congressional sweep. By the time Fox went on the air, Gingrich was the Speaker of the House and the country's most influential Republican. Roger Ailes is a man who places a high premium on access, and Hannity's closeness to Newt was an important link.

Hannity was not a complete TV virgin. In Atlanta he had done guest spots for CNN and occasionally he did a talking head gig at CNBC. But the medium felt new to him, and uncomfortable. "The first time I was on television I had a panic attack," he says.

When Ailes started Fox, Hannity's lawyer, David Limbaugh, Rush's brother, called and suggested a tryout for his client. Ailes saw potential and hired Hannity to do a debate show with a liberal cohost. They tried out a few before settling on Alan Colmes.

Hannity's early performances were shaky and awkward. "Looking at them now makes me cringe," he says. He didn't even know how to read a teleprompter; he learned by watch-

ing and copying Brian Williams. But his most important tutor
was Ailes. He showed Hannity how to ask short questions instead of delivering speeches. He instructed him to be better
informed, "report instead of just talk." And, most important,
he imparted the practical lesson of *You Are the Message*.

"One morning during the Monica Lewinsky scandal, Roger
called me in and said, 'Every time we're together you smile,
but last night on the air you didn't show me that side of your
personality. You seemed angry, and you're not an angry guy.
Lighten up.' He said it in a fatherly way, and it stuck," he recalls. "It was the best professional advice I ever got. Roger
Ailes changed my life."

Hannity's television persona is, indeed, far less abrasive
than O'Reilly's. It is also much more predictable. O'Reilly is a
social conservative, but he can be a populist on economic issues and tends to be open-minded on foreign affairs. Hannity
only departs from Republican orthodoxy when he criticizes it
from the right. When critics accuse Fox News of being a
megaphone for Republican talking points, they are primarily
pointing (whether they know it or not) to Hannity.

With the morning nailed down, market closing time settled, and prime time dominated by a one-two punch, Ailes had
one more key casting issue. He wanted a serious Washington-
centered news hour that could hold its own against the networks
and the cable competition, led by someone with unquestioned
mainstream media credentials, an outstanding professional
reputation, and a conservative outlook. There weren't many
of those, but Ailes only needed one, and he found his man at
ABC News.

Brit Hume did not boast a blue-collar pedigree. As a boy he
attended St. Albans prep school in Washington, DC, where
his classmates included Albert Gore Jr. Hume matriculated at
the University of Virginia and then followed what was, back

then, the usual route to journalist stardom: a stint at a wire
service and at a daily newspaper, the *Baltimore Evening Sun*.
He worked as an investigative reporter for syndicated columnist Jack Anderson and went on to ABC News, where he covered Congress and the White House. As an out-of-the-closet
conservative, he sometimes clashed with left-leaning anchor
Peter Jennings, but their relationship was mostly amicable.
Hume is not the sort of man whose integrity is easily questioned. Bill Clinton, with whom he had an occasionally contentious relationship, hailed him when he left the White
House press corps in 1996 for doing an "extraordinary, professional job under Republican and Democratic administra-
tions alike."

Hume and Ailes first met during the 1988 presidential
campaign, which Hume was covering for ABC. "Roger wasn't
a schmoozer, but he wasn't afraid of reporters, either. He
came at things as a straightforward political pro." Nothing
like a friendship developed, but they knew and respected each
other.

In 1996, Hume's ABC contract was up for renewal. He
wanted to stay, but not as the White House correspondent.
He flew up to New York and met for lunch with ABC News
president Roone Arledge. It didn't go well. "Roone was in a
distracted mood. He spent much of the lunchtime dumping
on Rupert Murdoch," Hume recalls. Presumably Arledge
raised the topic because Hume's wife, Kim, had left ABC
News to start as Fox's Washington bureau chief. Arledge told
Hume he was welcome to stay at ABC, but he wouldn't get
what he wanted—a more senior job as an analyst or anchor.

Hume left the lunch and considered his options. He admired CNN for its commitment to twenty-four-hour news,
but he considered it an amateurish operation. He was more
drawn to Fox, which was still in the planning stage. "I saw

what Roger had done at CNBC, turning it into a great franchise. And I knew Rupert Murdoch a little bit. When he hired Roger I remember thinking, 'I hope I hear from these guys.'"

He did. Ailes came to Washington, DC, in March 1996 and offered Hume the position of managing editor of the Washington bureau and a gig as anchor of the six o'clock news program, the Fox News "broadcast of record." He would be up against Peter Jennings, Tom Brokaw, and Dan Rather, the network Big Three. Hume was, he recalls, "thrilled."

Hume's first years at Fox were spent building a competitive newsroom staff in a journalistic environment that saw Fox as shaky at best and probably disreputable. It was a hard lift, but he had faith in Ailes. "That first year, Roger concentrated mostly on just getting up and running. He didn't seem upset at all by the low ratings; he was willing to give it time. After that first year, he acted like, "All right, now that I have time to raise the ratings, I will. And he did."

When the Monica Lewinsky story broke, the six o'clock show was still in the planning stages. Kim Hume recalled the way ABC's *Nightline* had started out as a series of "Special Reports" on the hostage crisis in Iran. She suggested using that name and launching immediately. Hume called Ailes in New York, and was startled when he said, "Sure. Let's start tonight." It was, Hume says, "an amazing risk," and it paid off. Fox *Special Report* built its eventual long-term success on its aggressive coverage of the scandal. Would Fox have been so eager to launch this type of news show had the president been a Republican? Hume says he isn't sure. Ailes, for his part, was delighted to have his six o'clock problem solved. After that first show, he called Hume and said, "ABC, eat your heart out."

Fox News was now up and running. Ailes had his team. Now he was ready to take on the world.

CHAPTER SEVEN

CABLE WARS

When Fox News started out, it got a generally skeptical and unfriendly reception from the journalistic establishment. Even reporters, who generally view any news media organization as a good thing (not to mention a potential source of employment), were largely disapproving. But no one greeted Fox News with more pure vitriol than CNN founder Ted Turner.

"I look forward to crushing Rupert Murdoch like a bug," Turner told the press. He compared Murdoch to Hitler, which would make Roger Ailes a reincarnation of Goebbels, and followed up with an explanation, quoted by the *Los Angeles Times*: "The late Führer, the first thing he did, like all dictators, was take over the press and use it to further his agenda. Basically, that is what Rupert Murdoch does with his media. . . ." The Nazi analogy was too much for the Anti-Defamation League, which rebuked Turner for trivializing the Holocaust. Turner apologized, but that didn't prevent him from likening Murdoch to "the late Führer" a year later;

or, in 2005, comparing the success of Fox News to the rise of Hitler.

Turner did more than call names. Having sold CNN to Time Warner, he was a member of the Time Warner board. Time Warner operated one of New York's two cable systems; the other belonged to the municipal government. As a condition of the sale of CNN, a federal antitrust suit required Time Warner to offer its subscribers a second all-news channel. Turner used his influence to make certain that this would be MSNBC. This choice would have kept Fox News invisible in the nation's media capital and ensured its failure as a national news organization.

Mayor Rudy Giuliani, a former Ailes client, stepped in and threatened to take action, even raising the possibility of allowing Fox News to use the city's cable system. Giuliani's opponents pointed out that his wife (now ex-wife) worked at the Fox broadcast affiliate. Giuliani insisted his motive was to keep a new TV channel, which provided hundreds of jobs, up and running. Suits and countersuits followed, there was an acrimonious debate in the press, and eventually a settlement was reached. Time Warner Cable agreed to carry Fox News in New York City by October 1997 (and elsewhere by 2001). It was a sweet victory for Ailes and Murdoch over CNN, and it wouldn't be the last.

Ailes likes to say that he has been up against eleven heads of cable news networks—six at CNN and five at MSNBC. Tom Johnson of CNN loomed the largest. He was the man Ailes needed to surpass to reach number one.

Johnson, like Ailes, came from a political background. After a brief career as a reporter for the Macon *Telegraph*, he earned an MBA at Harvard and worked for President Lyndon Johnson at the White House. When President Johnson retired to Texas, he took Tom Johnson with him, putting him in charge of LBJ Broadcasting, a company that included a TV station, KTBC in Austin. KTBC enjoyed a very profitable run as the monopoly station in Austin during the years Johnson was Senate majority leader and vice president. It made him and his wife, Lady Bird, very rich. In an irony the cynical Johnson would have appreciated, KTBC is now a Fox affiliate.

After the death of his patron, Tom Johnson served as publisher of the *Dallas Times Herald*, and then moved on to the *Los Angeles Times* as president and publisher. Ted Turner hired him in 1990 to run CNN. The timing was good. The first Gulf War was a high-water mark in Atlanta, and Johnson presided over the network for a decade.

"Ted found many of Rupert's business practices reprehensible," says Tom Johnson. The feeling was, of course, mutual. But Johnson did his best to keep out of the cross fire. "My job was to focus on running CNN. I left the Ted-Rupert battles to them." CNN under Johnson never lost its lead to Fox; he had the good luck to leave in 2001. "If I had stayed, Roger would have rocketed past me," admits Johnson.

In an effort to stay ahead, Johnson hired Rick Kaplan, one of the great producers in television history, to head CNN domestic news. Kaplan had many successes at ABC but one exploitable weakness: his friendship with Bill Clinton. When Kaplan came to CNN he brought this baggage along with more than forty Emmys. Ailes immediately dubbed CNN "the Clinton News Network."

"Roger knew I wasn't skewing the news for Clinton," says Kaplan. "But I was a friend of Clinton's, and how do you prove a negative?" Of course, Ailes was even closer to Clinton's predecessor, George H. W. Bush, but everybody knew Ailes had worked for Bush in 1988 and helped him in 1992. Kaplan was supposed to be neutral. Kaplan called Ailes and complained that his own mother was upset by the Clinton News Network jibes.

Ailes offered to call Kaplan's mother and explain that he wasn't trying to be nasty; it was only business. Kaplan thanked Ailes but assured him that "my mom will never take your call."

Nothing Kaplan did could stop the rise of Fox, and one of his mistakes cost CNN dearly. In 1998, as president of CNN-US, he oversaw the production of a new documentary magazine, *NewsStand*, which was billed as a synergistic *Time* magazine–CNN project. The first show, narrated by the New Zealand American journalist Peter Arnett, purported to be an exposé of U.S. troops using deadly sarin gas against civilians in Laos during the Vietnam War. The story was bogus. The network launched an internal investigation, which led to the firing of two producers and the resignation of a third. Arnett himself left soon thereafter. Tom Johnson issued a formal apology for allegations "that cannot be supported." Throughout the affair, Roger Ailes remained publicly silent. There was no need to rub it in. CNN was supposed to be the responsible cable network, Fox the tabloid partisan. The fiasco in Atlanta spoke for itself.

There was another aspect to Ailes's silence. He and Tom Johnson were close. "Roger and I represent two completely different political points of view, and we practice two different forms of journalism," says Johnson. "At CNN we made the news the star; Roger's style is more sizzling. I loved the competition. It improved us both, and it made CNN more aggressive. But—and this will surprise a lot of people—I enjoyed my personal friendship with Roger Ailes."

Johnson takes Ailes's claim to do "fair and balanced" news seriously. "CNN does a superb job with its hard news reporting," he says, "but I think that Fox does a very credible job. I see a rightward bias on the talk shows, but not in their coverage of events."

Despite their public rivalry, Ailes and Johnson sometimes quietly collaborated on matters of mutual importance. "Whenever one of our staffers got into serious danger in some of the world's reporting hellholes, we always watched after one another's personnel," Johnson told me. During the Balkan conflict, he learned that American stealth bombers were going to strike a Serb television station. He contacted Ailes and advised him to get his people out of the way. Johnson also prevailed on General Wes Clark to cancel the operation, which would also have killed Chinese, Russian, and other foreign reporters. It was only when all the international correspondents had left that the station was demolished, with several Serb fatalities. On another occasion, CNN personnel in Iraq were threatened and forced to leave. Ailes quietly shared Fox footage with his rival.

■ ■ ■

"The 2000 election was a turning point for Fox News," says Rick Kaplan. "Roger figured out that the country was at war politically, and that's how he played it. We didn't see it that way. And 2000 was the year that everything changed for CNN."

Conservatives voted with their TV remotes throughout the campaign, and stuck with Fox on election night. It was Fox that first called the election for Bush, and other networks followed suit. The decision didn't hold, and weeks of uncertainty followed. Although the issue was finally settled for Bush by the U.S. Supreme Court, Fox and the others had blundered with their premature announcements. Not only that, but by calling the result while some polling places were still open in Florida's central time zone, Fox News had risked compromising the election.

After that fiasco, Ailes went down to Washington to participate in a congressional grilling. "Fox News acknowledges here that it failed the American public on election night and takes full responsibility for this failure," he said. "These errors have led to much self-examination of the processes we used on election night, how the Voter News Service operated on election night, and our membership in the Voter News Service. Through our self-examination and investigation we have determined that there was no intentional political favoritism in play on election night on the part of Fox News."

The statement was self-serving and self-evident, like those of the other network chiefs. What mattered is that Ailes was in the company of Tom Johnson, his old nemesis Andrew Lack of MSNBC, and senior representatives of the Big Three broadcast networks. It was a sign that Fox News had arrived at full parity. A few months later, Ailes had the additional satisfaction of learning, via a vote count conducted by the *New York Times*, that Bush *had* won in Florida. To paraphrase Dan Rather on a different matter, the call had been journalistically wrong but factually correct.

The 9/11 Al Qaeda attacks on New York and Washington ushered in another Fox milestone. Other networks seemed unsure of how to deal with the shock of radical Islamic terror, but Ailes had no doubt. He immediately stocked the network with hawkish talking heads, many from the military; displayed American flags in the network's graphics; and began wearing an American flag lapel pin, a symbol that was adopted by on-air personnel. This gesture offended some mainstream journalists, like Av Westin, who broke into television journalism under Edward R. Murrow and became a senior figure at CBS, then ABC. "At ABC I had a rule—no campaign buttons in the newsroom," he told me proudly. The rule was supposed to ensure objectivity. Perhaps it did. It also obscured the fact that virtually everyone at ABC News was a liberal Democrat.

Some members of the network old guard protested to Ailes. At a media gathering in New York City, Morley Safer of *60 Minutes* laid into him for allowing his people to wear their patriotic sentiments on their lapels. "I'm a little bit squishy on killing babies, but when it comes to flag pins I'm pro-choice," Ailes replied.

In fact, the wearing of American flag pins was voluntary at Fox. Like the other networks, Fox didn't and doesn't allow campaign buttons.

While other networks looked for a balance between journalistic detachment and the patriotic mood of the country, Ailes was a supporter of the wars in Afghanistan and Iraq. "He sent word that we have to cover both sides fairly, but not to be ashamed to want America to win," says anchorman Bret Baier. He also sent a note to President George W. Bush encouraging him (as a private citizen, he later said) to hold massive public support for the war by fighting it in an uninhibited way. "The only thing America won't forgive you for is under-reaching," he wrote. At the time, Ailes was far from the only supporter of the "war on terror." Senior Democrats, including former president Bill Clinton, favored invading Afghanistan and Iraq. The Democrats in the Senate endorsed both wars. A great many mainstream media organizations fell into line. And, of course, Republicans enthusiastically supported the president. Polls showed that an overwhelming majority of Americans were with the president. But Ailes remembered Vietnam, where sentiment had turned around, largely due to the media. All three of the TV networks, led by Walter Cronkite at CBS, turned against the war after 1968. Thanks mostly to Fox News, no monopoly of mainstream networks and like-minded reporters now wields that kind of unchallenged influence or power.

■ ■ ■

In January 2002, Fox surged ahead of CNN, and never looked back. It soon outpaced CNN and MSNBC combined. A record number of people were watching cable news, and all three channels were covering basically the same stories. It was a chance for the public to compare the three, and the Nielsen numbers revealed that they preferred the Fox product. This was greeted with dismay and anger on the left. Within a year, Al Franken, Michael Moore, and a slew of journalists published anti-Fox books. Franken's was titled *Lies and the Lying Liars Who Tell Them: A Fair and Balanced Look at the Right*, and had a picture of Bill O'Reilly on the cover. O'Reilly went ballistic and insisted that Fox take legal action. Ailes complied, but a federal judge threw out the suit on the reasonable grounds that the book was protected by the First Amendment and that Fox couldn't plausibly claim ownership of the term "fair and balanced." The publicity around the case helped make Franken's book a national bestseller, and set him on the road to winning a Senate seat in Minnesota.

More than politics or patriotism was at work in Fox's rise to preeminence. "Roger is one of the few visionaries in the television business," says Rick Kaplan, who faced Ailes not only at CNN but later as head of MSNBC. He found fighting Ailes to be a punishing experience. "At times, I felt like Muhammad Ali up against Joe Frazier," he says. On the screen Ailes, with his flashy graphics, bumper music, constant controversies, and nonstop promotion, was more Ali than Smokin' Joe. Up against him, CNN seemed plodding and staid. "Roger understood cable news before anyone else. He realized that it isn't like broadcast news, an hour or two a day. It's a twenty-four-hour operation, which means that a good part of it has to be about opinions. At CNN we tried to do a 24/7 'broadcast of record' but it didn't work."

"This is a fifty-fifty country," says Chris Wallace. "There is no reason that Fox should get two-thirds of the cable news audience. A liberal tilt isn't inherently boring. But Fox is more entertaining and more interesting, and that's because of Roger. If he took over any network it would instantly become more successful. He's the most interesting figure in broadcasting."

A lot of outside critics agree. "Ailes cultivates his outsider persona. His charismatic stamp is all over Fox News," says Professor Richard Wald, the former president of NBC News and "ethics czar" at ABC News, and now a professor at the Columbia School of Journalism. "Suppose Bill Moyers was a libertarian. Change him from Lyndon Johnson's boy to Barry Goldwater's boy, but with the same unctuous personality. He wouldn't have been able to attract an audience." Luckily for Moyers, PBS evidently doesn't care.

"Fox is the ultimate surrender of news to entertainment," says Mark Danner, a professor of journalism and politics at Berkeley and one of the country's leading progressive intellectuals. "Ailes pioneered the unembarrassed consequences of the recognition that news is entertainment. His influence has been so great that it is now hard to recognize it. For example, the use of music intros and outros to the news is now so common that it goes unnoticed. Roger Ailes started it.

"Everyone I know in Berkeley or New York thinks watching Fox News is total insanity. Liberals look at the *New York Times*, or CBS, and see the news they offer, ideologically, as 'middle-of-the-road.' Fox, on the other hand, maintains that it is always in the opposition, even when Republicans control the White House or Congress or both. To the right, certain

permanent 'constituencies'—the entertainment and culture
industry, elite news media, and permanent bureaucracy—will
always be against them even when [the right] holds power.
This is how Ailes can seriously argue that it is Fox that is moderate and middle-of-the-road. He sees these permanent cultural and governmental forces as inherently liberal, and, seen
from this point of view, there is a good deal of truth to that."

Danner envies the energy Fox and others in the news
media have brought to the struggle. "In the 1960s, the energy
came from the left's positions on race, poverty, and opposition to the war in Vietnam. In 1976, as I went off to college, I
believed we were on the cusp of the era of liberalism." Four
years later, Ronald Reagan was in the White House, "and a
three-decade ascendency of conservatism began—and it con-
tinues. And of course those on the right, from Reagan on-
ward, basically believe that those sixties problems have been
solved," Danner says.

Danner's experiences with left-wing media, like Air America and MSNBC, where he is a frequent commentator, have
left him pessimistic. "I don't see a true liberal answer to Fox
on the horizon, although MSNBC tries hard," he says. "The
problem is that Fox, even now, is still more fun to watch.
Ailes has proved cannier in seeing what attracts attention. In
that sense, he's a transformational figure."

As Fox became more established, Ailes began moving it toward the journalistic mainstream. He carved out hours that
adhere strictly to broadcast news standards. *Special Report*
gave Fox viewers a place to go for a daily broadcast of record
at 6:00 p.m. In 2002, Ailes hired Greta Van Susteren away
from CNN and gave her the 10:00 p.m. slot. Van Susteren, a
lawyer, was highly regarded by the media establishment in
Washington, and her defection to Ailes came as an unpleas-
ant surprise to Fox's critics.

The following year, Ailes made an even more important acquisition when he hired Chris Wallace. He was broadcast royalty, the son of the legendary Mike Wallace—perhaps the greatest investigative interviewer in television history—and the stepson of Bill Leonard, the president of CBS News when CBS was the glory of liberal journalism.

Chris Wallace himself was the model of a modern major media figure. He had been a moderator of NBC's *Meet the Press* and then, for fourteen years, a senior correspondent and anchor at ABC News. When he announced that he was going to Fox in 2003, he imagined his colleagues would be critical of the move. Some were, but he was surprised to see that most understood the pragmatism behind his decision. "People at ABC knew that the network would never be as good as it was, that it was constantly managing the decline," Wallace told me. "The business model of a network with fewer and fewer viewers wasn't promising. Fox was growing. And it was entertaining. I discussed it with my father, who had been a great fan of Roger's for years, and he encouraged me to go ahead."

Ailes was delighted. Wallace had the sort of awards (three Emmys, a DuPont, and a Peabody) that made his mainstream credentials unassailable. He offered Wallace the job of hosting Fox's Washington Sunday morning talk show—Rupert Murdoch's favorite program—on two conditions. "Roger told me, 'I want you to be equally tough on Republicans and Democrats. And I want to know if you can get up in the morning and not think that America is to blame for most of the world's problems.'" Wallace assured Ailes that he could deliver on both counts, and went on the air in early December 2003. "Whether you like it or not," he recently told a gathering of journalists in Washington, DC, "Fox News is a major force in American journalism."

CHAPTER EIGHT

GARRISON

In 2002, Roger Ailes and his third wife, Beth, bought three (and gradually twelve) acres of land on a mountaintop overlooking the Hudson River, across from West Point. For much of his life Ailes had been a nomadic bachelor moving from station to station, campaign to campaign. Finally, at sixty, he was ready to put down roots.

Roger met Elizabeth Tilson at CNBC, where she was the director of daytime programming in charge of business news. When Ailes arrived to take over in 1993, she was the one who did the introductions with the staff. In time, he promoted her to vice president and she launched America's Talking.

Beth didn't follow Ailes to Fox. She had a one-year non-compete clause in her NBC contract. They did meet from time to time. "We were friends," she says. "Roger was in the process of getting divorced." Beth had been married before, too. Gradually their friendship escalated. Her sister Eileen encouraged her. "He's a guy who can tell you what to do and you can do it," Eileen said. Beth told me this with a laugh; she says her sister meant it in a flattering way.

Even after the courtship commenced, Beth took it slowly.

"At first I wasn't thinking of marriage," she says. "I was just glad to go out with someone who would pick up the check besides me." But soon enough they became a couple. On Christmas Eve 1997, Ailes said to her, "Let's go get a ring."

Beth said, "Great idea." They went to Tiffany's and selected an engagement ring. Rudy Giuliani performed the wedding at City Hall on Valentine's Day in 1998. After the ceremony and a reception, they took their families, Chet and Dottie Collier, and a midwestern friend named Bob Gordon, to dinner in a private room at Windows on the World. They went to Florida on their honeymoon to visit Ailes's mother and stepfather.

Beth, who is twenty years younger than her husband, wanted children. So did Ailes. In 2000, on New Year's Day, Zachary, Zac for short, was born. There had been a lot of concern at the time about what was called Y2K, that computers might not function because they hadn't been programmed for a change in millennia. The Aileses lived in Manhattan in an apartment on the thirtieth floor and worried that the elevators might stop running, leaving them stranded. Beth spent the evening resting on Ailes's couch on the second floor at the News Corp building and fought her way through the New Year's Eve traffic around Times Square to reach the hospital.

Like her husband, Beth Tilson grew up in straitened circumstances. She was one of five children raised in Watertown, Connecticut, by a widowed mother without a high school education who managed to send all of the kids to college. Beth majored in journalism at Southern Connecticut State. Her first job was as a production assistant at Satellite News Channel, a television version of 1010 WINS news, and from there she went to NBC. In a twelve-year career, she was promoted six times, and left the network shortly before Ailes did.

It took the Aileses four years to tame their wild property and reconstruct an old Yankee barn into a nine-thousand-square-foot home built of indigenous Adirondack river stone. "When we first started, the architect asked what kind of place we wanted," says Beth. "I told him that we are round, warm people and we wanted the house to reflect it." The interior is a combination of grand and homey: a marble foyer, mahogany floors, French country-style rugs and furnishings, an open floor plan, and river views from every room. "A lot of people in our situation would have had a team of decorators," Beth told me during a tour of the house. "But I did this myself. Roger has wonderful things that he's acquired over the years. But he wasn't very interested in the decor. His thing was, 'Just get it done.'" Ailes's only request for their home was for a circular dining table, eight feet in diameter. "I've been to a lot of dinner parties at rectangular tables where you get a deadhead next to you and you're stuck," he told me. "With a circular table, you can always talk to people across from you."

The Aileses do a lot of entertaining. Karl Rove, Rush Limbaugh, Rupert and Wendi Murdoch, Jon Voight, and John Bolton have been among their houseguests in Garrison. On Zac's ninth birthday, they threw a bash for 150 guests. The kids rode festively decorated ponies around the estate while Irish tenor Ronan Tynan serenaded guests including Rupert Murdoch, Rush Limbaugh, Bill O'Reilly, Greta Van Susteren, and other luminaries and friends. "Roger and I are both producers, and we put on parties like shows," says Beth.

■ ■ ■

I drove up to Garrison, about an hour and half from Manhattan, on a chilly Saturday morning in mid-January. The house is set back from the road, protected by a large security gate. A Christmas wreath still hung on the gate, near a sign warning visitors that the property is under video surveillance. I was buzzed in and found Roger and Beth waiting for me outside on the circular driveway. Ailes's burgundy 1985 Cadillac Seville trophy car was parked nearby.

Ailes is a military history buff and the first thing he pointed out was the spot where George Washington chained off the river to block the British advance in the Revolutionary War. Moving to the banks of the Hudson provided Ailes with a piece of Americana right outside his window. It was also a solid investment. As a small boy in Warren he was given a piece of real estate wisdom—always buy property on the water—which has remained a guiding precept.

Four years ago, Ailes took Zac to visit his boyhood home in Ohio. Zac stood in the living room and said, "This is smaller than our car."

"I told him my parents raised three kids here, and it was sufficient," Ailes says.

The centerpiece of the house is a mahogany-paneled library the size of a small basketball court. There are photos of heroes, some predictable (Generals Eisenhower, Patton, Lee, and Grant) and some less so (FDR and David Ben-Gurion, Israel's socialist founder). There is also a photo of Ailes in the Oval Office with Richard Nixon, taken on the day Neil Armstrong walked on the moon. "I produced the conversation between Nixon and Armstrong," he said. "It was the first broadcast between earth and space." The walls are lined with books. Ailes, a collector, keeps first editions in a special closet. He showed me a biography of Stonewall Jackson. During

World War I, a young officer named George Patton owned the book and scribbled his comments on General Jackson's tactics in the margins.

Up a flight of stairs, on a table near the picture window, sit two urns that contain the ashes of Ailes's mother and step-father. "They were cremated in Florida and when we went down there I didn't like the looks of the place, so we took them with us," he says. He and Beth were on the way to an overnight stay with Rush Limbaugh, and Ailes informed him that he would be arriving with his mother and her husband. He didn't tell Rush that he was bringing them in a gym bag, a discovery that disconcerted the host. Ailes brought them to Garrison and put them where they could see the Hudson. "My mother always wanted to live on the water," Ailes said in a not completely facetious tone.

■ ■ ■

Garrison, and the villages of Cold Spring and Nelsonville, technically belong to Philipstown, a metropolis of about ten thousand souls. The area was settled more than sixty years before the American Revolution, and for most of the time since then it has been a backwater. Its greatest pre-Ailes event was the train wreck of 1897, in which twenty people died. Ailes moved there imagining an idyllic, prosperous corner of small-town America where he would live among the sort of patriotic, God-fearing folks he identifies with. The military academy in nearby West Point was a visible symbol of the place he took the town to be. But Philipstown is no longer the village of his imagination, the sort of village that produces sons like Sergeant Hamilton Fish II, the first Rough Rider to die in Cuba during the Spanish-American War. There is still plenty of fighting spirit, but it is directed not against Ameri-

ca's external foes but developers who might want to despoil
Mother Nature. For many of his neighbors, these enemies are
embodied by Mr. Ailes and Fox News.

West Point is not the only landmark visible from Ailes's
window; he can also see Storm King Mountain, one of the
iconic sites of the modern environmental movement. In the
midsixties, the Scenic Hudson Preservation Coalition brought
a lawsuit to stop Con Edison from building a pump storage
generator and power lines there. The suit ended in a precedent-
setting decision that aesthetic impacts could be considered in
the licensing of power projects. Philipstown is now home to a
plethora of nature sanctuaries, interfaith retreat centers, bio-
ethics think tanks, Outward Bound USA, and numerous en-
viromental nonprofits. As Peter Boyer wrote in his *New Yorker*
piece about Roger Ailes and the area, "Preservation [is] the
local industry."

Not everyone in Philipstown is a progressive or an environ-
mentalist. Former New York Republican governor George Pataki lives there. So does Patty Hearst, the heiress/captive/
radical bank robber/society matron whose political status is
eternally unclear. The majority of townspeople are not particularly political. But Garrison and Cold Spring have their
share of Fox haters, for whom the arrival of Roger Ailes was
not a happy occasion.

Ailes's first response was to defuse the situation with dis-
plays of generosity and goodwill. He donated to local charities, drove his Caddy in the Fourth of July parade, shopped in
local establishments, and generally made it clear that he
wanted to be part of the community. But, being Ailes, he
didn't bother to hide his disdain for the local pieties or institutions. The nearby public school, for example, proved too
liberal and touchy-feely for his taste, so he enrolled Zac in a
Catholic school in Manhattan. And he complained about the

taxes, which, in his view, were out of proportion to the government services. He took to referring to the environmental establishment, with its heavy regulatory hand, as "the Politburo." None of this endeared him to the Philipstown gentry.

In July 2008, Ailes and his wife, Beth, bought the local newspaper, the *Putnam County News and Recorder*, a weekly broadsheet known as the *PCN&R* that had been in existence, in one iteration or another, since the administration of Andrew Johnson. The paper was a typical village gazette, filled with bland neighborly stories about local occurrences and people. Beth Ailes became the publisher (and after Roger sold his share to her for a nominal price, the sole owner). The *PCN&R* remained a studiously local paper, but it also began to change. She reinstituted the paper's original motto, "By the Grace of God, Free and Independent," began running excerpts from *The Federalist Papers*, and—most controversially—broke with tradition and began running editorials, including one critical of the administration's spending policies. There was, for the first time, actual reporting in the paper, including the disclosure, in a much-remarked-upon article, that some teachers and administrators in the 260-student Garrison Union Free School District were earning six-figure salaries.

Opinions in town vary over why Roger Ailes would want a local newspaper with an estimated readership of ten thousand. The anti-Ailes faction sees it as a vanity project or, more darkly, an effort to seize a partisan advantage. The notion that a man who runs two national networks would worry about Democratic Party control of Cold Spring and Garrison is a tribute to the self-regard of the community as well as the paranoia Ailes tends to arouse. He says he bought the paper "so the bastards couldn't roll me on taxes." But whatever his motives, the progressive opposition crystalized in the form of the Full Moon Project, a group dedicated to saving the town's civic virtue from the Ailes's family. What emerged was a website, Philipstown.info, owned and operated by Gordon Stewart, a Manhattan corporate executive, art collector, and sometime speechwriter for Jimmy Carter (he had a hand in writing Carter's infamous "malaise" address) who arrived in Philipstown a few years after Ailes did. Stewart—who, in an odd coincidence, roomed with Ailes's brother, Rob, at Oberlin College—grew up in Chicago as the son of poor Jewish immigrants, and in some ways, he says, he has more in common than Ailes does with the plain folks of his adopted (weekend) home. At first, he opposed the Full Moon idea of a rival newspaper, but he eventually changed his mind, setting up shop on Main Street. Ailes says that after Philipstown.info opened, a death threat was placed on the *PCN&R*'s door. Stewart dismisses this as a drunken prank. "Apparently someone tacked a message on the door of the paper. It was a bar-closing moment, and I had a long talk with the sheriff about it."

The *PCN&R* has established a policy of not mentioning Philipstown.info. Stewart finds this infuriating (which is, of course, its purpose) and he believes that it is a symptom of Ailes's high-handedness. "[Roger's attitude] is, we did all these wonderful things, held picnics, invited people up to the estate and they were ungrateful. But if you approach a hardscrabble yeomanry population from the stance that they are supposed to be grateful for your arrival, that you are beneficent and they are the local peasantry, that's not going to work, even if people are politically comfortable with you."

Actually, there is little reason to imagine that Ailes is unpopular outside of the artsy-émigré circle. When Philipstown proposed a new zoning plan, a hundred-page legal document that Ailes considered a landgrab, he brought in a lawyer whose services he offered free of charge to members of the "yeomanry." More than eighty people took him up on it. "The plan was too complex for the average person to understand," he told me. "And I don't like seeing rich environmentalists steal farms from old ladies." The plan was altered to satisfy most of Ailes's objections.

■ ■ ■

After Saturday morning brunch, Roger and Beth took me on a tour of the town. Our first stop was a nearby construction project; Beth and Roger, inspired, she says, by Rush Limbaugh's compound, are renovating a 1950s house for use as a guesthouse. The site was muddy. Getting out of the car, Ailes stepped in a puddle and said, "Damn, I'm ruining my good shoes." He seemed genuinely upset about the prospect of having wrecked what looked to me like a very nice, but not especially fabulous, pair of black loafers. Ailes is a city man; he does not believe that, in confrontation between a puddle and a man's shoe, the puddle should prevail. He also confided that he was afraid that Beth would be upset with him if he tracked mud into the house.

From the construction site we drove three minutes to Main Street in Cold Spring. At the end of Main Street, Ailes stopped so I could get a view of Dockside, formerly the site of a ramshackle restaurant that was bought and demolished in 1999 by the Open Space Institute and is now a passive-use park. "They took a place where a guy could sit and look at the water and drink a beer or eat a cheeseburger and turned it into a place for dogs to shit," he said. "How the hell is that an improvement?"

Ailes clashed again with the émigré establishment when a group of artists staged an exhibition of sculptures along the river. Ailes loudly derided the exhibition as an "eyesore."

"Roger has a commanding view of the marsh," says Stewart. "His attitude was, 'Look at all this ugly shit. They're only there because they don't pay taxes.'" Predictably, this didn't go down well with the local cultural institutions that sponsored the show. "Roger put them in an impossible position. He humiliated them. Why would he go out of his way to do this?"

The answer was: retaliation. For some time, local authorities had wrangled with Ailes over changes he was making on his property, which, in their opinion, disturbed the environment.

"They told me that I had runoff from my property. I explained to them that God made water run downhill, not me. But since I had just bought the land below my house, they had nothing to worry about anyway." When authorities tried to prevent him from putting a deer fence on his property, Ailes said that the fence was meant to keep the deer out of his flower beds and prevent his German shepherd, Champ, from killing the deer. He added that if any EPA inspectors came on his property to look for infractions, and there was no fence, the inspectors could also wind up as dog food. The fence is still standing.

The tour ended on Main Street, at the office of the *PCN&R*. The building has been restored by Beth to its quaint, early twentieth-century condition. An elevator has been installed for Roger, who has a hard time getting up and down stairs on his damaged legs. Even the anti-Ailes faction admits that the building is an improvement—no small matter in a town whose commerce depends, in large measure, on its pristine quaintness. As for the paper itself, it is, in the assessment of the *New Yorker*'s Peter Boyer, "distinctly better" than it was before Beth Ailes took it over. The new *PCN&R* hasn't destroyed the social fabric of the town or opened the way for wrong-thinking Republicanism, as the grandees of the town feared. What it has done is to give readers, yeomen and émigrés alike, a choice of news. It is a Hudson Valley version of fair and balanced, and if the liberals of Cold Spring don't like it, they have a lot of company all across the blue states of America.

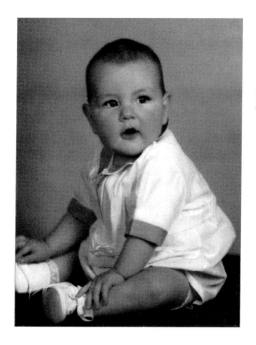

Roger Ailes, son of Warren, Ohio.

Bob Ailes and Donna Cunningham Ailes, Roger's parents, on their wedding day. They divorced when Roger was in college.

Bob and Donna Ailes with their three children, Robert Jr. (Rob), Roger, and Donna Jean (Jeannie), at home in Warren.

Roger Ailes at sixteen. Despite suffering from hemophilia, his dream was to become a combat pilot.

Out of college, Ailes started working for *The Mike Douglas Show*. He became executive producer of the show at age twenty-five. From left to right: Roger Ailes, Mike Douglas, and Chet Collier.

In the 1970s, Ailes spent a few years as a Broadway producer. One of his plays, *The Hot l Baltimore*, won three Obies and a New York Drama Critics' Circle Award for Best American Play of 1973. Here, Roger is backstage at *The Night That Made America Famous* with composer Harry Chapin and actress Kelly Garrett.

Ailes and Richard Nixon met on the set of *The Mike Douglas Show.* Ailes later became Nixon's TV campaign producer and changed the way presidential politics was televised.

Ailes was called in to coach Ronald Reagan for his crucial second debate in the 1984 presidential campaign.

In George H. W. Bush's 1988 campaign, Roger Ailes was strategist, morale officer, and the producer of some of the most effective ads in political history.

Roger and Rupert, a partnership that revolutionized television news.

Ailes eased out Glenn Beck, replaced him with an amiable ensemble talk show, and kept control of the five o'clock slot. Here, Ailes is with members of Fox News' *The Five*. From left to right: Kimberly Guilfoyle, Bob Beckel, Andrea Tantaros, Eric Bolling, and Dana Perino.

Roger Ailes and Bill O'Reilly (here with pundit Monica Crowley). They turned the eight p.m. show slot into a goldmine.

Friendship before politics: Roger Ailes with Barbara Walters and columnist Liz Smith.

Former New York City mayor David Dinkins and Reverend Jesse Jackson at the 2012 graduation ceremony of the Ailes Apprentice Program. Jackson delivered the keynote address.

In 1998, Roger married Elizabeth Tilson. They met as colleagues at **CNBC**.

Roger with his only child, Zac.

CHAPTER NINE

FAIR AND BALANCED

When Roger Ailes rolled out Fox News, he gave it what he knew would be a provocative motto: "Fair and Balanced." Nothing he has done since has so inflamed his critics. Fair and balanced is what the mainstream media have always claimed to be. Laying claim to it mocked the pretensions of the establishment. If the slogan had accomplished nothing more, that would have been sufficient for Ailes.

It is an American tradition for media organizations to christen themselves with self-regarding slogans and mission statements. When legendary newsman Adolph Ochs took over the *New York Times* in 1896, he published a declaration of principles setting forth his goals, including "to give the news impartially, without fear or favor." He promised his readers "All the News That's Fit to Print." The *Chicago Tribune* vaingloriously dubbed itself "The World's Greatest Newspaper." The *New York Sun* boasted that "It Shines for All." Not to be outshone, the *Baltimore Sun* offered "Light for

All." The *Los Angeles Times* put "Largest Circulation in the West" on its masthead; the *Los Angeles Herald Examiner* trumped that with "Largest Circulation in the Entire West." The *Longview* (Texas) *Daily News* proclaimed itself "An Independent Democratic Newspaper of the First Class, Unchallenged in Its Field." In Nevada, the *Mason Valley News*, with a refreshing sense of proportion, still bills itself "The Only Newspaper in the World That Gives a Damn About Yerington."

Television network divisions have adopted their own identities. ABC News enables its audience to "See the Whole Picture." CNN is "The Most Trusted Name in News." MSNBC "Leans Forward."

Most subscribers to the *Chicago Tribune* didn't actually believe that theirs was the uncontested champion newspaper of the world. CNN, to judge by its ratings, is far from being the most trusted name in news. And not even the most fervent admirers of the *New York Times* suppose that *all* the fit news is found in its pages. These are understood to be aspirational statements, not literal fact. They are not ordinarily regarded as scandalous assaults on the truth.

"Fair and balanced" is different. Bill Keller, the former executive editor of the *Times*, wrote a column about it in May 2012, calling it "a slogan for the suckers" that intentionally masks the fact that Fox News, in its coverage as well as its commentary, is unfair and unbalanced, and outside the norms of conventional journalism. It was not Keller's first swing at Fox News and its founder. The previous year he told an audience at the National Press Club that "the effect of Fox News on American public life has been to create a level of cynicism about the news in general. I think it has contributed to the sense that they are all just, you know, out there with a political agenda, Fox is just more overt about it . . . the national discourse is more polarized and strident than it has been in the past." Keller was unaware at the time that the day's moderator, Marvin Kalb, the founding director of Harvard's Joan Shorenstein Center on the Press, Politics and Public Policy, was a contributor to Fox News. "My problem with Fox News isn't that it is conservative," Keller told me in a phone interview in the summer of 2012. "My problem is that it pretends not to be conservative. 'Trust us, everybody else in the media is liberal' is the attitude it takes . . . the tenor of Fox News is different."

Roger Ailes doesn't disagree that Fox is different from other news organizations. He often illustrates this point with a story about meeting a man at a cocktail party (presumably on the Upper West Side of Manhattan, although the venue changes in retellings) who complains about Fox News coverage. Ailes asks him if he is satisfied with what he sees on CNN, NBC, ABC, CBS, MSNBC, and PBS. The man says he is very satisfied. "Well," says Ailes, "if they all have the same take and we have a different take, why does that bother you? The last two guys who succeeded in lining up the media on one side were Hitler and Stalin."

■ ■ ■

"The first rule of media bias is selection," Ailes says. "Most of the media bullshit you about who they are. We don't. We're not programming to conservatives, we're just not eliminating their point of view."

All news organizations practice editorial selection. "News" is not an objective and empirically measurable outcome, like a baseball score or yesterday's temperature. As newspaper columnist Walter Lippmann famously noted, the world is full of activity. Editors and gatekeepers operate a searchlight, scanning the globe. When they spot something of interest to them, they pause to illuminate it.

The choice of what to illuminate is not self-evident, but somehow the mainstream media tend to arrive at a consensus about what does and does not constitute a story. This consensus, for national and international stories and cultural issues, has traditionally been set primarily by the *New York Times*, which is the morning newspaper of almost every network news executive. It is a cardinal principle at Fox to avoid doing this.

"We try to avoid pack journalism and concentrate on what is important to viewers," says Michael Clemente, executive vice president of news. "A lot of journalists feel that if they all do the same thing in the same way, they are safe. That isn't the case here. And we are less dependent on the *Times*."

"I was in key positions determining the news agenda at ABC and CBS," says Av Westin. As he sees it, the good old days are gone forever, thanks to Ronald Reagan (who ended government regulation of the airwaves), Rupert Murdoch (who brought British tabloid standards to television), and, of course, Roger Ailes. "Ailes arrived in this environment, and it was clear that he would do anything to get ratings," he told me.

According to Westin, TV was once in the hands of great, disinterested figures like CBS founder Bill Paley, and operated by public-spirited local station managers. This, of course, is preposterous. The networks were always corporations and they often intervened in the activities of the news division when they saw a threat to their corporate interests. For example, ABC altered a *20/20* story on used car dealer–insurance company scams because some affiliates thought it would offend sponsors, Westin says. Westin assured me that he never had a case in which news management imposed its political point of view. But there was no need. "We all batted from the left side of the plate," he says. Walter Cronkite, the "most trusted man in America," exemplified the myth of the neutral and politically disinterested television journalist. In a generally admiring biography of the avuncular Cronkite, published in mid-2012, historian Douglas Brinkley reveals the extent to which the CBS anchor was an active player in Democratic politics. In the wake of the book, NBC's Chris Matthews—another Democratic player in those days—confirmed the open secret of pervasive bias in the "golden age" in a speech at the National Press Club.

"The big networks for years had establishment liberalism as their basis of true north," he said. "That's what they were—Cronkite and Edward R. Murrow—establishment liberals. Everything was liberal, basically, but it was a point of view and they laughed at Goldwater. Cronkite mocked him with the way he pronounced his name . . . [Cronkite] had a point of view and we all knew his point of view. He was a liberal the whole time he was in television." Matthews thinks that despite this (or, perhaps, because of it) Uncle Walter was an honest reporter. But Matthews is a liberal himself. If Cronkite and the vast majority of television journalists had been conservatives, right-wingers probably would have considered them honest and fair.

Cronkite was venerated by other television journalists inside CBS News and beyond. His politics were not seen by them as an issue because they were shared. Westin told me that in his many decades in television news, he could recall only two senior journalists whose views ran counter to the prevailing ideology—Howard K. Smith, who supported the war in Vietnam, and Brit Hume, who was suspected of having a cozy relationship with President George H. W. Bush.

Matthews informed his audience that the days of reflexive and authoritative "that's how it is" TV journalism were over. "It's too complicated. It's too many points of view," he said.

"Today those points of view are more transparent, they're more acknowledged."

Journalists have a very hard time admitting, or even detecting, their own biases. But Ailes, by providing an alternative take, has made those biases obvious. For example, after Fox News scooped the *New York Times* by a week on the story of apparent malfeasance at ACORN that led to its bipartisan defunding by Congress, the *Times* found itself in the embarrassing and revealing position of assigning a journalist to monitor what was being reported by Fox News and other conservative news organizations.

Conservatives consistently and angrily denounce the *Times* as a left-leaning paper—a charge that is usually dismissed by its senior executives and journalists. "The *Times* isn't in anyone's pocket," Bill Keller told me. "We did a lot of tough reporting and published a lot of critical comment on Bill Clinton, Eliot Spitzer, and other liberal Democrats." This is a standard defense, but it misses the point. Of course the *New York Times* sometimes reports negatively on its favorite public figures and issues. So does Fox News. During the 2012 primary campaign, at least three of the losing Republican candidates accused the network of being in the tank for someone else. When President Obama announced his support for same-sex marriage, anchorman Shep Smith played the clip and said, "The president of the United States, now in the twenty-first century." A few minutes later, he asked Bret Baier if the Republican Party would do the same or oppose it, "while sitting very firmly, without much question, on the wrong side of history. . . ." And it was Fox that broke the story about George W. Bush's drunk-driving record a few days before the 2000 election. "Hell, that could have cost him the presidency, but we had it so we reported it," Ailes told me.

"One of the things that make Fox different is the way Roger

frames stories," says Rick Kaplan. "Take the issue of choice. On the broadcast networks, if they do a story they will probably center it on young girls and how hard it is for them to find an abortion provider. Roger might do the same story and focus it on adoption and how young girls can arrange one. That's the sort of conservative angle that broadcast news doesn't usually pick up on."

In the spring of 2012, the case against the *Times*'s liberal bias got an unexpected witness—Arthur Brisbane, the paper's own public editor. In a column he wrote that spring, Brisbane charged the *Times* with failing to cover the Obama administration with sufficient tenacity or skepticism (he noted that the newspaper's senior editors had even written a highly sympathetic biography of the incoming president). And in his valedictory column, at the end of August, Brisbane sharpened his indictment. He wrote:

> I . . . noted two years ago that I had taken up the public editor duties believing "there is no conspiracy" and that the *Times*'s output was too vast and complex to be dictated by any Wizard of Oz–like individual or cabal. I still believe that, but also see that the hive on Eighth Avenue is powerfully shaped by a culture of like minds—a phenomenon, I believe, that is more easily recognized from without than from within.
>
> When the *Times* covers a national presidential campaign, I have found that the lead editors and reporters are disciplined about enforcing fairness and balance, and usually succeed in doing so. Across the paper's many departments, though, so many share a kind of political and cultural progressivism—for lack of a better term—that this worldview virtually bleeds through the fabric of the *Times*.
>
> As a result, developments like the Occupy movement

and gay marriage seem almost to erupt in the *Times*, over-loved and undermanaged, more like causes than news sub-jects.

Brisbane concluded with praise for what he called Times Nation—loyal readers of the paper online as well as in print, all across the world. But he added a cautionary note. "A just-released Pew Research Center survey found that the *Times*'s 'believability rating' had dropped drastically among Republicans compared with Democrats, and was an almost-perfect mirror opposite of Fox News' rating. Can that be good?"

To Roger Ailes, it can be very good indeed.

■ ■ ■

A few weeks after Bill Keller publicly assailed "fair and bal-anced" as "a slogan for the suckers," Ailes retaliated.

In a speech at Ohio University, he called the *Times* a "cess-pool of bias," and its reporters "lying scum." He was reacting to a *Times* story written more than a year earlier by Russ Buettner about allegations that a senior News Corp executive had encouraged Judith Regan, the mistress of disgraced New York police chief Bernard Kerik, to lie to federal investigators about Kerik, who was being considered for the post of secre-tary of Homeland Security at the time. Kerik's patron (and Ailes's friend) Rudy Giuliani had presidential aspirations. Regan charged in a lawsuit that Ailes advised her to mislead investigators to protect Giuliani. Ailes recalls it differently, and his recollection is backed up by a letter from Regan af-firming that he did not try to influence her to lie about Kerik. Ailes thought the article on the matter, which the *Times* ran prominently, was unfair, and he used the speech in Ohio to settle a score. He later let it be known, via a Fox spokesman, that he regretted the remarks, although he never apologized publicly. He told me that he likes and admires Jill Abramson, the *Times*'s current editor in chief, whom he has known since she was a reporter covering the 1988 presidential campaign. Abramson wasn't the editor at the time of the offending article; Bill Keller was.

The *Times*, for all its flaws, is a great newspaper, self-critical enough to employ aggressive ombudsmen like Brisbane and willing to acknowledge specific mistakes. It is also open to occasional stories that depart from the general tone of the paper. I know this from personal experience. Several years ago I wrote a cover story in the *New York Times Magazine* on Rush Limbaugh; its lack of venom occasioned howls of protest from Times Nation, but Keller defended it as fair-minded (which it was, if I do say so myself). I never had any doubt that it would be published the way I wrote it. I agree with Keller that the *Times* has a certain kind of journalistic integrity "embedded in its DNA." As he put it, "Good reporters see it as part of their job to second-guess assumptions, including their own."

I heard Ailes say the same thing to a group of journalism students at the University of North Carolina. Of course, he was talking about different assumptions. "It is fine to question your country," he said. "But if you want to be a good reporter, you have to question the questioning, too." This sort of jujitsu is what infuriates liberal critics, because Ailes adroitly turns the clichés of their profession against them. Is the press skeptical? Then where is the skepticism about President Obama and his policies? Does it speak truth to power? Who, exactly, do liberals have to fear except the IRS and one another? "The entertainment industry, elite news media, and permanent bureaucracy all have an interest in large government," says Mark Danner. "This is the basis of Ailes's point that Fox is moderate and middle-of-the-road. He says the rest of the media are liberal, and there's a lot of truth to that."

One of the hallowed clichés of journalism is that the press's role is to "afflict the comfortable and comfort the afflicted." The phrase is often misattributed to H. L. Mencken, the most impious and least comforting of American journalists; it was actually coined more than a hundred years ago by the Chicago satirist Finley Peter Dunne, who put it in the mocking mouth of his fictional Irish character, Mr. Dooley:

> "Th newspaper does ivrything f'r us. It runs th' polis foorce an' th' banks, commands th' milishy, controls th' ligislachure, baptizes th' young, marries th' foolish, comforts th' afflicted, afflicts th' comfortable, buries th' dead an' roasts thim aftherward."

Setting aside Dunne's fin de siècle snark about newspapers, standing up for the afflicted is a good aspiration—when it is clear who is on the side of the angels, as it was during the civil rights struggle in the 1950s and 1960s. But very few conflicts in the contemporary world are so morally unambiguous. There are afflicted people on both sides of most political issues. Comfortable ones, too.

Ailes, of course, knows this. "Roger laughs at his critics and he mocks them," says Chris Cuomo, one of the hosts of ABC's 20/20, who went to work for Ailes at Fox News in 1996. "The idea that the rest of the media are straight down the line is hypocritical and silly. Does Fox have a different perspective than CNN? Sure. We all pick who and what we feature. But Roger makes sure that both sides get told. When he came out with 'We report, you decide' [another foundational Ailes slogan], I loved it. He came right at the criticism. Roger played the media for fools when he was a political consultant. He knows how they work. He doesn't pander to them and he isn't afraid of them."

From the outset, Ailes wanted to accomplish two things: He wanted a network that would appeal to conservatives and that had plausible deniability to the charge that it was a conservative organ. Given the state of American television journalism at the time, it wasn't hard to do, at least in comparison to the industry standard. In 1996, you could count the number of conservative talking heads and news commentators on one hand. PBS had William Buckley; CNN used Bob Novak and Pat Buchanan (who did double duty on the *McLaughlin Group* syndicated talk fest); ABC empaneled George Will on its Sunday morning interview program. A few conservative commentators did guest spots (Ailes did some himself on NBC), but they were almost never on without a rebuttal by a liberal (and often more than one).

This imbalance presented Ailes with two golden opportunities. First, he was able to scoop up most of the really good conservative talent—Charles Krauthammer, William Kristol, Fred Barnes, Brit Hume, and Bill O'Reilly. At the same time, he hired lots of mainstream journalists and liberal commentators, whom he put under exclusive contract, including Susan Estrich, Alan Colmes, Juan Williams, David Corn, and others. They took hits from their colleagues for consorting with the enemy, but Fox actually paid its contributors well— an attraction to talking heads of any ideological persuasion— and they argued that they were, by going on Fox, changing conservative minds. Some left-wing critics charged that Ailes hired weak progressives and threw them to the right-wing wolves; Al Franken dismissed Colmes as "loofah-ing Roger Ailes in his personal steam room." Ailes took the stance that he hired bona fide liberals; if they couldn't make their points effectively, that wasn't his fault.

One offshoot of Fox's success is that it has paved the way for right-wing commentators on other networks. They are still in the minority—"there are more liberals on Fox than all the networks combined have conservatives," says Brit Hume—but it is now considered necessary to have somebody articulating conservative viewpoints. In an interesting turnabout, hard-core right-wingers now dismiss David Brooks (*New York Times*, PBS, National Public Radio), *Washington Post* columnist Kathleen Parker (who had a short-lived debate show with Eliot Spitzer on CNN), and MSNBC host Joe Scarborough as fainthearted faux conservatives.

Fox, in the meantime, has continued to stockpile liberals, twenty-four at last count. Among them are former Clinton adviser Kirsten Powers, who often appears on *Special Report*'s "Fox All-Star" panel; former Democratic senator Evan Bayh of Indiana; and Joe Trippi, the political consultant who managed Howard Dean's presidential run. Of course, the game is rigged. Powers is outnumbered two to one by conservative fellow panelists. For every Joe Trippi there is a Dick Morris *and* a Karl Rove. Bayh is an eloquent centrist, but he lacks the star power of Sarah Palin. But Ailes didn't invent these rules; he simply turns them against his competition and in doing so he has given conservatives what they never had on any network: a home court advantage.

It's not that Ailes has achieved (or wants to achieve) real ideological or partisan parity. His liberals are there by and large for the same reason conservatives are at the other networks, as foils and tokens. It may be true, too, as Rick Kaplan says, that the conservatives on other networks are better than Fox's liberals. That's a matter of taste, and not the point. Ailes has made it disreputable to exclude right-wing analysts and commentators, or to frame the news too much. "Roger widened the agenda," says Dick Wald. "It would not be better if the three networks and Bill Moyers were the only choices. Journalism is better for having opposing points of view."

Fox may or may not be internally balanced. But Ailes is right when he says, "Sometimes we *are* the balance."

■ ■ ■

"I don't think Rupert Murdoch ever *told* Roger what to do," says Av Westin. "He wouldn't have hired Roger if he didn't know that Roger was on the same page." Westin is absolutely right. "Roger has strong views and vice versa," Rupert Murdoch told me the first time we spoke. "He is longer and wiser in politics than I, but we broadly share the same views. There was nothing we had to agree on before I took him on board." This is a very concise formulation of the normal proprietor-editor relationship.

It also describes the relationship between Roger Ailes and the six thousand or so people who report to him. Time and again, Fox journalists assured me that Roger Ailes has never told them what to say on the air or how to report a story. This is something you hear not only at Fox, but from self-respecting journalists throughout the media. And it is true, up to a point.

News organizations work like every other kind of hierarchic bureaucracy. "Let's face it," says Westin, "we all get our jobs through peer group selection. The people who were in charge of promotions moved me along. I pitched the right stories. And who will you pick [for a promotion]? Someone out of the same mold." In other words, if you hire and promote people who share the general views and ethos of their workplace and are keen enough to see where the lines are, there is no need to tell them what to say or, in this case, report.

Unlike most other news organizations, Ailes has not had the luxury of choosing his personnel from a large pool of like-minded candidates. Polls taken over the last forty years consistently show that the great majority of journalists identify as liberals and vote for Democrats in national elections. Fox hires conservative Republicans, but there are not enough of them to stock a network. "Most of our producers are liberals," says Michael Clemente, the vice president in charge of news. He was the executive producer of ABC's *World News Tonight* during Peter Jennings's tenure as anchorman and, before that, a senior Washington producer for CNN. His pedigree is strictly establishment—he worked with David Brinkley and Barbara Walters, and describes himself as nonpolitical. The reason why Fox has so many liberal producers isn't ideological or political; it is a matter of necessity. "We're in New York, after all," he says. Fox also has a fair number of reporters who lean to the left in their personal views. It is fair to say that Fox News is more to the right than its staff, but it turns out that it is also closer to the left than Roger Ailes.

■ ■ ■

Tim Groseclose is a professor of political science and economics at UCLA. He is an Okie with the country twang and conservative views to prove it, and he also happens to be one of the best-trained and most highly regarded social scientists in the country. Groseclose, working with Steve Levitt of *Freakonomics* fame and James Snyder of Harvard, devised a method for measuring the political quotient (PQ) of politicians. The general idea is to take congressional members and place them on a liberal-conservative continuum based on the ratings of the Americans for Democratic Action, a Democratic-leaning organization. For example, Michele Bachmann and Jim DeMint are near zero—the most conservative. Nancy Pelosi and Barney Frank are close to 100. President Obama, according to his estimates, is about 88. Not surprisingly, the average voter is close to 50.

Next, Groseclose computes the slant quotients of news outlets. To do that, you take the on-the-record speeches of congressmen and senators and examine which think-tank sources and other authorities they quote approvingly. Then you compare these with the think-tank sources and other authorities quoted approvingly in news stories. This gives you a slant quotient (SQ) for the aggregate news stories in each media organization. The average Fox show had, in 2004, an SQ of about 40, which places the network about 10 points right of center. All the other television news programs Groseclose examined were left of center (i.e., had an SQ greater than 50). *PBS NewsHour* was the most moderate, with an SQ of 55. The nightly news shows on the broadcast networks all hover around 65. This makes intuitive sense: Mainstream network news shows differ mainly in the personality of the anchors.

Groseclose then attempts to compare the leanings of mainstream journalists to the content of their reporting. Surveys consistently show that the great majority of mainstream reporters vote for the Democratic candidate in national elections. This was very likely the case in 2008, a supposition President Obama acknowledged at his first White House Correspondents' Dinner when he laughingly told the audience that "most of you covered me, all of you voted for me. Apologies to the Fox table."

Professor Groseclose puts the PQ of the average political reporter for a mainstream organization at 95, very close to the president's, but the slant quotient of their news organizations, he finds, was closer to 65. In other words, the conventions of journalism meant their reporting was roughly 30 points nearer to the center than their own views.

Groseclose's analysis relies on data that predate the second Bush term and the Obama administration. I asked him if he has detected a change. "Based on my casual observation, the slant of Fox between 2004 and 2008 was no different than its slant before 2004," he says. "In 2009, however, it seemed to have moved slightly to the right. The biggest change was that the *Hannity & Colmes* show became the *Hannity* show. I'd say the change represented something like 25–35 points on my slant quotient scale. Otherwise, I don't think there has been much of a change at Fox. Greta Van Susteren's show, again based on my casual observation, changed from being slightly left-leaning centrist toward being slightly right-leaning centrist. Shep Smith's show seems to have moved the opposite— from slightly right-leaning centrist to slightly left-leaning centrist. *Special Report*—whether hosted by Brit Hume or Bret Baier—remained right-leaning centrist. If anything, Baier seems to have moved the show slightly closer to the center [i.e., leftward] than it was with Hume."

In his book, *Left Turn*, Groseclose provides a ten-question test that enables anyone to arrive at a personal political quotient. I tried it myself and came up with a score of 55, which puts me somewhere between Republican moderate Chris Shays of Connecticut and Blue Dog Democrat Ben Nelson of Nebraska. I invited Roger Ailes to take the test as well. He hesitated—his political views are too nuanced, he said, to show up correctly on a test—but eventually he agreed. His score was 25—fifteen points to the right of the news coverage on Fox, somewhere between Jack Kemp and Ron Paul. Ailes didn't disagree. "I am more conservative than the network," he said. "That's true. And I do influence things here. But I don't dictate."

■ ■ ■

Ailes often complains that his views are misrepresented by journalists who haven't spoken to him. "In forty years, no reporter has ever actually asked me what my position is on any issue," he says. So I asked what Ailes would do if he were president. "I could never be elected," he said. "I couldn't follow my own advice. Duck, weave, that's what a candidate needs to do. That's not me. I'd probably start calling people jerks. So, I wouldn't be a viable candidate."

He also admitted that he wouldn't be suited to holding a political office. As a teenager he was chosen to represent Warren G. Harding High School at the Buckeye Boys State, an annual assembly. "I was elected president pro tem of the senate, and I found it very boring," he said. "In a negotiation I can always sit and outwait the other guy, but I have a very short attention span for things that irritate me."

So the White House is out of the question. But, as a hypothetical, what would an Ailes administration look like? "I'd start by repealing some of the laws we have that are unnecessary or worse," he said. "The country doesn't need more laws and regulation, it needs less."

"Social Security and Medicare are more or less grandfathered in," he says, but he would get rid of the Affordable Care Act and slash new federal entitlement budgets. "Teaching people dependency is a sin," he told me. There is only one entitlement Americans need—the opportunity to live in this country.

Under President Ailes, taxes would fall and budgets would be slashed. "You can't get anywhere bargaining over spending programs with the Democrats," he says. "Whatever you offer, it isn't enough. Say three billion and they demand nine. When you say no, we don't have the money, they portray themselves as generous and us as stingy. That's a trap we shouldn't fall into."

Unions, which Ailes considers job killers, would not have a friend in the White House. Neither would what he calls "extreme" environmentalists. "I want clean water and clean air and conservation," he says, "but that's not what extreme environmentalists are all about. For them it is a religion. They believe in trees and animals, not God."

When it comes to foreign policy, Ailes is a hawk who believes in supporting friends all the way and spending whatever is needed to preserve American military supremacy. "Strength breeds peace," he says. "Nobody walks into a bar and picks a fight with the toughest-looking guy in the place," he told me. At the same time, he thinks his party has a tendency to underestimate the value of diplomacy. "There are deals that can be made, and should. It was a mistake to use the phrase 'for us or against us.' Of course, you maintain your core policy principles. But within each one of these is a broad range of practical conservative solutions. I'd hesitate to say this at a conservative gathering, but I think conservatives are sometimes too rigid."

As an example of an exercise in mutual self-interest, he offers Vladimir Putin's unwillingness to help the United States bring down the Assad regime in Syria. "Putin is angry. He thinks the United States doesn't take him seriously or treat Russia as a major player. Okay, fine, that's how he feels. If I were president, I'd get in a room with him and say, 'Look at the slaughter going on in Syria. You can stop it. Do it, and I'll see to it that you get *all* the credit. I'll tell the world it was you who saved the innocent children of Syria from slaughter. You'll be an international hero. You'll go down in history.' Hell, Putin would go to bed thinking, 'That's not a bad offer.' There will still be plenty of other issues I'd have with Russia. But instead of looking for one huge deal that settles everything, you take a piece of the problem and solve it. Give an incentive for good behavior. Show the other guy his self-interest.

Everybody has an ego. Everybody needs dignity. And what does it cost? You get what you want and you give up nothing."

Give-and-take is a principle Ailes lives by, a politician's way of looking at the world. There is no chance that he will ever put it into practice in the White House. But it is an insight into how he conducts his business in the only house that really matters to him, the House of Ailes.

CHAPTER TEN

THE BOSS

At precisely two thirty in the afternoon, Roger Ailes walked down the hall from his office to the meeting room. Eight men—seven of them white—and one woman, all middle-aged and dressed in business attire, were gathered around the polished table. The room is functional, not fancy. The rear wall holds a battery of television screens silently showing all the cable news channels. The only art is a poster with a quotation from Thomas Jefferson that Ailes likes: "If I had to choose between government without newspapers, and newspapers without government, I wouldn't hesitate to choose the latter." Sometimes visiting delegations meet with Ailes in this room; he serves them sandwiches and soft drinks and jokes about his girth. But there were no refreshments at this meeting. Ailes loosened his tie, draped his jacket over the back of the chair, and eased himself into what is, literally, the seat of power at Fox News. It is from here that Ailes exercises his influence, and the executives gathered at the table are what he sometimes calls, with only the faintest hint of irony, his "loyal lieutenants."

The two-thirty meeting is one of two that take place every day. The first is at 8:00 a.m., an hour when Ailes is sometimes taking his son to school. On those mornings he is present via speakerphone. Zac sometimes pipes up with a question or story suggestion, which delights Ailes. "He'll probably be a vice president by the time he's twenty-one," Geraldo Rivera once told me.

Like his prime-time talent, Ailes's executive lineup doesn't change much. He prizes loyalty and competence, and once he finds them he holds on. Bill Shine, the man who some think will be Ailes's eventual successor, has been at Fox since the beginning, working first as the producer for *Hannity & Colmes* and now in his current post as senior vice president for programming. Shine, like Hannity, is a Long Island kid from a lower-middle-class background. He attended a SUNY college and broke into television at WLIG-TV, a New York–area CBS affiliate. It was Hannity who brought him to Fox.

Shine has the job of managing the vast egos of some of the Fox stars, as well as riding herd over about a hundred paid commentators. He is plainspoken and sharp-witted: When Ailes introduced me to the group as a writer working on a book about Fox News, he winced theatrically and said, "Write this down. My name is John Moody."

I sat next to Michael Clemente, a large, open-faced, slightly unkempt man who, I noticed, refrained from laughing along with the others. In 2009, Clemente replaced Moody as vice president in charge of news as a part of Ailes's well-publicized repositioning toward the center. Moody was moved to a job as head of the experimental News Corp in-house wire service. Clemente discontinued the controversial daily memo, but he sees nothing wrong with it. "I worked at ABC and CNN and

I have friends at the other networks, and they all have variations on a memo. What company doesn't?" Clemente holds his own meeting at seven thirty each morning, and then monitors the stories in progress during the day.

Ailes nodded to Clemente, who gave a very quick rundown of the day's news and where things stood. He began with the death of right-wing media provocateur Andrew Breitbart, whose scoops had recently brought down Congressman Anthony Weiner and helped precipitate the defunding of ACORN. Just a couple of weeks earlier, at the conservative CPAC convention in Washington, he had promised to display hidden tapes from Obama's Harvard years with allegedly damning material. The AP was reporting that Breitbart had keeled over around midnight while walking the dog near his home in Los Angeles.

"How old was he?" asked Ailes.

"Forty-three," said Clemente.

"They're going to do an autopsy?"

Clemente said he didn't know.

"When somebody threatens to use tapes like that, it can cause a lot of stress," said Ailes. "Talk to his family. And find out where the tapes are and what's on them." (The tapes emerged a few days later; they were innocuous, Obama introducing a left-wing Harvard law professor, Derrick Bell, to a student demonstration.) "What's next?"

"Mixed economic news from General Motors and Ford today," Clemente said.

Ailes turned to Brian Jones, head of news operations for Fox Business Network. "How are those little electric cars doing?" he asked. It was a rhetorical question—everyone knew they were selling poorly.

"Have we done any business stories on building new cars in the North and the South?" asked Ailes.

Jones said no, not lately.

"Everyplace that has unions is doing lousy; the places where there are no unions are doing fine," Ailes said. "Maybe somebody should go out to Trumbull County and ask, Would you rather have a union and be out of a job or vice versa?"

Clemente said, "Not much else. There was an Internet outage at the Pentagon today."

"What was that all about?" asked Ailes.

There were shrugs around the table. Computers, cyberspace, these things happen. . . .

"How long did it last?"

"About half an hour," said Clemente. "From what I understand, they got it fixed."

"Wait a minute," said Ailes. "There has to be an explanation. Get our Pentagon people on this. I want to know what caused this. Where in the Pentagon, what systems were affected, what part? Could something like this happen when incoming missiles were on the way? Did the critical systems go down?"

Clemente said he would get on it.

Back in his office after the meeting, Ailes shook his head over the equanimity with which the Pentagon outage had been accepted. "If a screen goes dark at Fox for half a minute I have the engineers up here explaining what the hell happened. I want to know what show of ours was on at the time, what shows were on the other networks. And that's television, not goddamn national security." Ailes is sometimes accused by his critics of not being a journalist, but he has a keen sense of skulduggery, honed by his years in politics. "I didn't come out of news, I came out of life," he says. "People will always come to rest if you let them. My job is to keep asking questions."

The meeting shifted to Bill Shine and the subject of candidates appearing during primary season. The night before, Mitt Romney had appeared on *The O'Reilly Factor*. Ailes said, "I thought Bill was a little overboard fair to Romney."

"Bill explained to him what he should be doing," said Shine drily.

There were chuckles around the table. Ailes said, "Just be sure that he's fair with Santorum tonight." Shine made a note. A few weeks later, with the primaries going Romney's way, Senator Santorum accused Fox—where he had formerly been employed as a commentator—of being in the tank for Romney. Ailes thought that was silly. "I don't have a favorite," he told me later. "I know them all." During primary season, most of the Republican candidates, including Romney, paid courtesy calls on Ailes. Ailes also did his own scouting. He and Rush Limbaugh invited Governor Chris Christie of New Jersey to dinner in Garrison to explore his political plans. Christie is a candidate cut from the Ailes mold—blunt, funny, knowing, dedicated to small government and practical solutions—and although Ailes promised him nothing, he liked Christie. Limbaugh did, too. But in the end, the governor didn't run.

The voice of Bill Sammon, the Washington, DC, managing editor, came from the speakerphone on the table. "We've got an interview with some guys from the first U.S. commando unit, in World War II—they were the basis for Tarantino's *Inglourious Basterds*," he said.

"Wasn't that the story of the Richard Burton movie, *Devil's Brigade*?" Ailes asked.

Sammon, who is a generation younger than his boss, said he had never heard of *The Devil's Brigade*. (Sammon was wise not to yes-man his boss's memory; Ailes was wrong. *The Devil's Brigade* starred William Holden.)

Ailes told the group that he had received a note from Barbara Walters asking if Sarah Palin, now a Fox contributor, could appear as a guest on *The View*. This was a sore point. Walters is an old friend, but Palin had embarrassed Fox News by announcing her decision not to run for president on a rival radio talk show. In the end, Ailes didn't have to decide. Palin, who felt her family had been slandered on the program, told ABC that she had no intention of appearing on the show.

Kevin Magee, the Fox Business News executive vice president and former vice president in charge of radio, raised his hand. Magee has been with Fox for ten years. Before that, he was a producer at CNBC and ABC. "CNN radio is shutting down," he said.

"CNN radio is shutting down?" Ailes repeated. Shep Smith once told me that the only thing more important to Ailes than beating CNN is CNN losing to Fox: "I wouldn't say he wants everyone over there dead, but it's close."

Cheered by the good news, Ailes raised the subject of Syria. Marie Colvin, an American reporter for the British *Sunday Times,* had just been killed by a bomb while covering the siege of Homs, and he wanted updates on the situation there. "Jesse Jackson called me today," he said. "He wants to go to Moscow and protest the Russian government supporting Assad. I told him that we'd look into the possibility of coverage. We have to open a new front in Syria or a shitload more people will die. Assad's murdering journalists and silencing them. It's troubling when a country goes silent. Somebody talk to Walid Phares [a Fox Middle East commentator] and let's find out what the terrorists are up to over *here* these days. Somebody get in touch with Ray Kelly about it." Kelly is the New York City police commissioner. He is also the father of Greg Kelly, an anchorman at the Fox affiliate in New York, which is supervised, like all the affiliates, by Ailes.

The two-thirty meetings are a function of the news of the

day. Ailes throws out ideas, but he doesn't usually insist. No Fox News crew visited Trumbull County to find anti-union autoworkers. He wanted to make a general point, not order a specific story. But that happens, too, usually via *Fox & Friends* or *The Five.*

In mid-March, Clemente had come in with a column that had been published that day by David Ignatius in the *Washington Post.* Ignatius reported having seen Al Qaeda documents, including a message from Adam Gadahn, the Al Qaeda media adviser to Osama Bin Laden, on how best to disseminate a video celebrating the tenth anniversary of 9/11. Clemente read aloud: *"It should be sent for example to ABC, CBS, NBC, and CNN and maybe PBS and VOA. As for Fox, let her die in her anger."*

"That's great," said Ailes.

"There's more," said Clemente. *"From a professional point of view, they are all on one level—except Fox News channel, which falls into the abyss as you know, and lacks objectivity, too."*

"We should put this up on a billboard in Times Square," said Ailes. Ailes is famous for putting up billboards, but there was no need.

A couple of hours later on *The Five,* Greg Gutfeld, one of Ailes's favorite comedians and a rising star at the network, read the memo and added that it "sounds like it was written by Media Matters."

Ailes had come from a big lunch and he had walked in yawning, but the Gadahn memo picked him up. "What else do we have?" he asked. Clemente said that the government's numbers on inflation had just come out. Many conservatives suspect that the Obama administration has kept the index artificially low. "We should figure out the actual costs for a middle-class family," Ailes said. "My God, it costs hundreds of dollars a month just to feed a family. Hell, a kid can go through a box of cereal in no time. You know what a box of cereal costs?" He didn't wait for an answer. I guessed that he probably knows. He once told me that his mind automatically registers small details. "I pass a Lowe's on the way home," he said. "I look at the parking lot and notice how many cars are there compared to how many there were last time. It tells me how the local economy is doing."

Brian Jones made a note to look into it. Clemente added another tidbit. "George Clooney and his father were arrested protesting outside the Sudanese embassy in Washington," he said.

"The *dad*!" said Ailes. "That's sick."

Bill Sammon was on the speakerphone again. He mentioned the developing case of parents who filed a wrongful birth suit against a physician who failed to alert them to the fact that their child would be born with Down syndrome. "Wonder how the kid will feel when he grows up and finds out about it," Sammon said. Heads nodded in agreement. Abortion is one of the subjects that Ailes feels strongly about, and he doesn't keep his view to himself. Around that time, Ailes was interviewed by hip-hop mogul Russell Simmons on his podcast. Simmons asked why Hispanics seem to be overtaking African Americans as the most influential ethnic group of color. Ailes snapped that it is because so many African American mothers abort their babies.

This afternoon Ailes wasn't in the mood for a discussion of moral philosophy. The night before, he had watched a pop culture quiz on *The Factor* that pitted Steve Doocy against Brian Kilmeade, his cohost on *Fox & Friends*. "They got every single answer wrong," Ailes said. "I don't know what that was. Maybe it was O'Reilly trying to make them look bad. We should look into it." I thought he might be kidding, but Shine made a note of it.

Ailes had a couple more items on his agenda. He reminded everyone that electrical work was being done in the "Brain Room," the sexy name he has given to what is the Fox research computer center. "They say it has to be rewired," he said darkly. "Fine. But I want the name of everyone who goes in there." He was also concerned about the possible ill effects of Internet social media being used as reliable sources on the air.

"Tell our young producers to be careful about what we put on the screens. And round up five or six people in the building who know the most about social media, put them in a room, and ask them what they know that we don't know. Make it an hour discussion and I want to see a report on it. Oh, and tell the young producers that the screen needs refreshing. I'd give a bonus to them for higher ratings. We have to incentivize them. Meals or something."

Ailes was yawning again, and twiddling his thumbs as the various vice presidents discussed their activities. But he perked up again when Magee reported that NPR was retracting a story it had run on Apple's allegedly inhumane treatment of Chinese workers. Ailes does not like National Public Radio, which he considers the epitome of political correctness—and worse, correctness underwritten, at least in part, by his taxes.

Ailes had a chance to strike back at NPR in 2010. Juan Williams was a correspondent for National Public Radio; in fact, it later emerged, he was the only black male on the air. He was also a commentator on Fox News. It was in that capacity that he appeared one night on *The Factor*. "I'm not a bigot," he told Bill O'Reilly. "You know the kind of books I've

written about the civil rights movement in this country. But
when I get on the plane, I got to tell you, if I see people in
Muslim garb and I think, you know, they are identifying
themselves first and foremost as Muslims, I get worried. I get
nervous."

Williams had gone on to say that this sort of concern
should not be a reason to discriminate against Muslims. But
NPR didn't pause to listen to that part. He was a respected
author, an Emmy winner, a former *Washington Post* columnist, and a contributor to prestigious publications like the
New Republic, the *Atlantic Monthly,* and *Ebony.* But he
worked for Fox News, which made him, in the eyes of a certain kind of liberal, a heretic. Many at NPR had been longing
to settle accounts with him. He was fired over the phone without an explanation or a chance to defend himself. NPR issued
a statement saying that Williams's remarks were inconsistent
with its editorial policy. Two days later, NPR president Vivian
Schiller told an audience in Atlanta that Williams's feelings
about Muslims should be between him "and his psychiatrist,
or his publicist—take your pick." In other words, Juan Williams was either a bigoted paranoiac or a money-grubbing op-
portunist.

Schiller's statement was hard to defend, and NPR didn't
try. She apologized to Williams, but the NPR board vetoed
her annual bonus and pressured her lieutenant, Ellen Weiss,
a close friend of Hillary Clinton, to resign. A few months later
Schiller was fired after another NPR senior executive was
caught on video, by the right-wing videographer and activist
James O'Keefe, disparaging Christians and Republicans to a
prospective donor from a fictional Islamic organization. Schiller was subsequently hired by NBC as its chief digital officer.
Juan Williams, meanwhile, was bailed out by Roger Ailes.

The firing of Juan Williams was a public scandal, but it

was also a personal crisis. "Let's say I had a sleepless night," Williams told me. The next night on his show, Sean Hannity noticed that Williams was not his usual self. Williams told Hannity what had happened. Hannity called Bill Shine at home, and Shine took it to Ailes. The following day Ailes invited Williams to come to his office. "When I walked in, Roger was sitting in a chair in the corner, and he said, 'We can't have you working here, can we?' And then he laughed." Ailes offered Williams a contract that would compensate him fully for the money he had been making at NPR. "I don't want you to have to go home and tell your wife you lost something," said Ailes.

The banter and the generosity were part of a relationship that went back to the days when Williams was a young correspondent during the Reagan administration; Ed Rollins (who now works for Ailes as a commentator at Fox) made the introduction and they hit it off. "Roger was a source during the first Bush administration," Williams says. "He paid attention to me, this young, skinny black kid, and made sure I was in the loop. It would have been easy for him to ignore me or mislead me, but he didn't." Of course, Ailes had a good reason to get on good terms with a reporter, regardless of how young, who was covering politics for the *Washington Post*. But Ailes understood that young journalists need to feel validation. "People like Larry Speakes [the White House spokesman] preferred to deal with more senior correspondents. Roger had a different attitude. It was like, 'You and I are fellow underdogs. If you can't find something out, give me a holler.' I felt like, at some level, the connection was personal."

In 1996, Ailes called Williams, who was a substitute host at CNN's *Crossfire*, and offered him a job as a commentator. "My wife was against it. Leave the brand name? But I believed in Roger and in 1997 I went over. I knew that Fox leaned to the right. It was clearly antagonistic to Clinton during the impeachment trial, and in the 2000 election it was closer to Bush than Gore. But there I was, on the air, voicing contrary opinions to Hannity and O'Reilly. A black man who works for Fox is suspect. I was disrespected for it at NPR, even though I was working for Fox when they hired me. But there are a lot more blacks at Fox than there are at NPR. I was the only black man on the air, along with maybe four women. MSNBC and CNN are very short on black talent. Under Roger, at Fox, there is more opportunity."

When Williams came aboard full time in 2010, Ailes was delighted. Not only did he have himself a first-rate full-time commentator going into election season, he also got a chance to call the NPR's leaders "the left wing of Nazism." It was a phrase too far, and it engendered a rebuke from the Anti-Defamation League's Abe Foxman. Ailes "apologized" for using the term "Nazi" to describe the leaders of NPR "when in my now considered opinion 'nasty, inflexible bigot[s]' would have worked better. . . . Juan Williams is a good man and like you, a friend. And my friends never have to worry about me sticking up for them—even if I'm occasionally politically incorrect, I never leave any doubts about my loyalty."

CHAPTER ELEVEN

THE GIFT OF FRIENDSHIP

One of the first people Roger Ailes hired at Fox News was a young reporter named Douglas Kennedy. It raised eyebrows: He was the youngest son of Bobby Kennedy, born a year before his father was assassinated by Sirhan Sirhan in Los Angeles while campaigning for the Democratic presidential nomination. The Kennedy family business is politics, but Doug decided to go into journalism. He started out at the *Boston Herald* and then came to New York as a crime reporter for the *New York Post*. Although he didn't have much television experience, he put together a reel of appearances and sent it to Chet Collier at Fox. Kennedy came on board as a reporter a month before Fox launched.

"Some people at the network resented it and some still do," he said. "I've had epic battles at Fox where my name was an undercurrent," he says. He was protected, then and now, by Roger Ailes.

"Some people find their own humanity overwhelming.

Roger doesn't. He knows you when he is talking to you. You walk by Roger in the hallway and he's happy to see you—not the fake TV executive happy, but genuinely. He grabs you by the shoulders and there you are, wrestling with him in the corporate office building."

Kennedy is a lifelong Democrat. "I was terribly moved by the election of the first black president," he says. Ailes was less moved, but it doesn't matter. "What people don't understand is that Roger is very comfortable with others who don't agree with him. He knows what he believes and says it— Roger never talks for effect—and we go out to lunch and really go at it. All he asks is that you be real with him in return."

After Kennedy went to work at Fox, liberal friends suggested that Ailes was using him for public relations, to demonstrate Fox's fairness and balance. "That's never happened," he said. His family stood behind his decision to work for Ailes. In the midseventies, "Roger took my brother Bobby to Kenya and made a wildlife documentary," he says. "It was a kind gesture on his part. In my family, Roger is held in high regard. We don't think of him the same way others in the Democratic Party do."

The African excursion came up at lunch with Austin Pendleton. Ailes's version was far different from Doug Kennedy's account of Roger as an avuncular benefactor. He said that he had a client with $100,000 in hard currency that the Kenyan government wouldn't allow out of the country. The client came to Ailes and asked if he could use his political contacts. Ailes had a better idea: He offered to produce a documentary film with the money and then sell it to American television. That way, everybody came out ahead.

The question was, Who would buy a nature travelogue? What would the hook be? "I needed an automatic sale," Ailes told Pendleton. "At the time, there was no name more commercial than Kennedy. And I knew Bobby Jr. was a wildlife guy." Ailes took the proposal to Lem Billings, an intimate of JFK and after the assassination of Bobby Kennedy a mentor to his sons. Billings wasn't sure it was a good idea, especially given Ailes's Republican credentials and his work for Nixon, but he promised to raise it with Ethel Kennedy. Ailes waited several months while he was vetted, and finally got a yes. "We can't find anyone who says you are untalented or a liar," Billings told him, "so you can go ahead if you promise to protect Bobby." They shook on the deal, traveled to Kenya, and made the film, which recouped the client's money with a tidy profit.

Sometime later, I informed Doug Kennedy that Ailes's motive for making the documentary had been financial, not humanitarian. He just laughed. "Roger always wants people to think he is worse than he is," Kennedy said. "He hates admitting that he's softhearted."

I had noticed this myself. He often talks about epic fights that, on closer examination, turn out to be more like scuffles, and he usually explains his motivations and behavior in the most cynical way. When I asked him why, he began by denying it.

"What I told you and Austin was the truth. I did want to find a way to get the money out of Kenya. And it worked. But, yeah, there was more to it than that. Bobby was a troubled kid. He was obnoxious at the beginning of the trip, too. He borrowed a comb from the cameraman and then tossed it on the ground. I took him aside and said, 'Pick up the comb and hand it to the cameraman. He's going to be filming you for the next month and if you act like a prick, he's going to make you look like one.'"

Over the course of the trip, though, Ailes took a liking to Kennedy. "One night Lem Billings and I were sitting around the campfire—we were the last ones awake—and he said to me that Bobby would be running for office eventually and he wanted my promise that I would help him. I told Lem I couldn't guarantee that—I didn't know what the political situation might be in the future. But I did promise that I would never work against him, for a candidate who was running against him. And I promised I would always look out for Bobby."

The Kenyan expedition resulted in a decadeslong connection between the Kennedy clan and Ailes. Ailes is especially close to Ethel, whose charities he has supported over the years. He was also friendly with John Jr. They had several meetings in Ailes's office to explore joint marketing strategies for Fox News and Kennedy's magazine, *George*. After one of those meetings, Ailes walked JFK Jr. through the Fox newsroom so he could say hello to Doug. "The girls down there were practically fainting," Ailes recalls. He offered Kennedy his own talk show on Fox. Kennedy was considering it when his plane went down.

After the birth of Doug Kennedy's fifth child in the winter of 2012, he tried to take his infant son out of the hospital to get some fresh air. Two nurses intervened, and they got into a scuffle. Since it involved a Kennedy, the incident became a sensational story. Reporters flocked to the hospital in northern Westchester; news helicopters flew to the scene. "In my family the reflex in a situation like this is to shut up," Kennedy told me. "But Roger said, hell no. Fight! Nobody touches your baby. Stick up for yourself. You did nothing wrong."

Ailes instructed Kennedy to leave the hospital and come to his house in Garrison. Beth cooked him dinner. Ailes told the press that Kennedy had been right to do what he did. "You don't grab a baby out of the arms of a loving father," he said. (A Westchester court subsequently acquitted Kennedy of all charges.) He was, needless to say, grateful for Ailes's support.

"There is no other television executive in the business who would do something like that," he says. "No one."

In the winter of 2012, Ailes, Beth, and Zac took a short vacation to Palm Beach. One night Ethel Kennedy invited them to a small party at her estate, where he found himself surrounded by friendly Kennedys and other liberals. The next day he took Zac to hang out with Rush Limbaugh in his studio. "I doubt if too many people have had a weekend like that one," he says.

Chris Cuomo is another scion of a liberal Democratic dynasty, the son of former New York governor Mario Cuomo and brother of the incumbent, Andrew Cuomo. He considers Roger Ailes one of his close friends. They lunch often, and discuss personal problems and professional issues. "I was at CNBC when Roger began staffing Fox News," he told me. "I was twenty-eight, just starting out. When Roger hired me he said, 'I don't care who your father is. Just do your job the right way.' He's a guy's guy, a brilliant teacher, and as good a boss as I've ever had. If he wanted me to come to Fox, I'd be tempted."

The roster of Friends of Roger is long and incongruous. It includes Rudy Giuliani and Gladys Knight, Jack Welch and Jesse Jackson, George H. W. Bush and Dukakis campaign chief Susan Estrich. Dennis Kucinich, the former boy-wonder mayor of Cleveland and longtime darling of the progressive wing of the Democratic Party, is a buddy. When he and his wife came to Garrison for dinner, Ailes saw to it that a photo of Kucinich and Elizabeth made the local paper. "I wanted the local commissars to see it," says Ailes. "I thought it would ruin their day." He regularly lunches with Henry Kissinger. He was so close to Geraldine Ferraro, the Democratic vice presidential candidate on the Mondale ticket Ailes helped to defeat in 1984, that he produced a film of her marital rededication ceremony. He also hired her as a commentator on Fox and, when she was diagnosed with cancer and couldn't work, kept her on the payroll at full salary.

It is easy to be cynical about Ailes's friendships, many of which double as business connections or professional relationships. They undermine the notion, fostered by Ailes himself, that he is hated by the liberal establishment. "There are some who think Roger would love to be the subject of scorn and abuse, but he isn't," says Rick Kaplan. "The truth is, in our business he is admired—I love Roger Ailes." Kaplan doesn't hold a grudge over Ailes's disparaging comments about the Clinton News Network. Cable news, Ailes style, promotes itself through controversy and personal feuds, but— like politics or boxing—only suckers believe the contestants actually hate their opponents.

Once Ailes makes friends, he tends to keep them. When he began the second round of his television career, he brought in Chet Collier, his old mentor in Cleveland, as his second-in-command. And he remained close to his first boss at *The Mike Douglas Show*, Woody Fraser.

Douglas died in Los Angeles in 2006 at age eighty-one. His widow called Fraser and asked if he would be willing to put together a memorial show. Fraser wasn't enthusiastic. A few years earlier he had been asked by the widow of Steve Allen, Jayne Meadows, to stage a similar tribute. It was a flop. "Steve Allen had been a beloved figure in the show-business community in Hollywood," Fraser told me, "but despite that, almost nobody agreed to show up. Everybody had an excuse— they were out of town, they had a crucial appointment, something. Really, most of them just didn't want to bother. And Mike Douglas wasn't Steve Allen. He wasn't especially well liked in L.A. I got some of the original staff on board and we tried to get some of the guests on the Douglas show to appear, but when we called around, people kept turning us down."

Fraser called Ailes and told him what was happening. "We need names," he said.

Ailes saw this as a debt of loyalty. He told Fraser to send him a list of celebrities who had been guests on the show, and he began to work the phones. "Just about everybody on that list, from Tiger Woods to Billy Crystal, showed up," Fraser said. "Roger came, too, and gave a speech. The show went really well and afterward Roger took me aside and said, 'I'd forgotten what a good producer you are.'"

The job offer came with a caveat. "This may not work," Ailes said. "I once worked for you. Now this is my ship and it works my way. You can't break legs here. I have ten executives who have made Fox News number one, and if you don't get along with them I'll have to let you go."

Fraser took the job but the adjustment wasn't easy. He clashed with some of the Fox brass, especially John Moody, the executive vice president in charge of news. "Moody and I didn't like each other," Fraser says. "He told me that I didn't know anything about news. I told him that I had produced *Nightline* and *Good Morning America*. He wasn't impressed, and I wasn't impressed with him." The antipathy got nasty and it was talked about at the network.

Ailes does not abide internecine warfare. It was a negative situation, and negative situations, according to him, make positive people sick. He called in his old boss and read him the riot act. Fraser promised to be good. "I'm proud of Roger," he says. "He taught me something important. I wish I had learned before how to work with people without breaking legs."

Anyone who has any experience with Ailes knows that he prizes loyalty, to him and to the company he runs. Violate it, and you wind up like anchorman Mike Schneider or Jim Cramer, out on the street looking for a new job. But abide by it

and you have a supporter of uncommon power and understanding. For example, Ailes recently sent a young reporter
from an affiliate, who had had a fistfight in the newsroom, to
anger management. "If you run an organization and nobody's
crazy, you never get a full picture of life's possibilities," he
says.

"Roger taught me that being a great interviewer is a mixture of head, heart, and balls, and even if you have all three,
you have to figure out how to use them effectively on the air,"
says Chris Cuomo. "A lot of TV journalists are afraid to do
that."

When Geraldo Rivera was expelled from Iraq amid charges
that he had endangered American lives in wartime, a lot of
news executives would have been glad to see him go. Ailes
was different. "Roger totally backed me," Rivera says. "He
stuck up for me with the Pentagon, and he was steady as a
rock. We are both smart guys who push back. Roger has a lot
of physical courage and it gives him his swagger." A few weeks
after telling me this, Rivera ran into Ailes and repeated the
quote, to which Ailes replied, "Damn right."

"Ours is a perfidious business," Cuomo told me, "but Roger
stands up for his people. When somebody threatens to sue a
Fox reporter, Roger comes to that person and says, "'Are you
right on the story?' If you say you are, he believes you and
then the people complaining have to get through him."

"Roger thinks long and hard about hiring, but once you are
in, he's got your back," says Chris Wallace. "He's never told
me who to have on the show or what questions to ask. But loyalty is very important to him. I found that out."

In the spring of 2008, Wallace did a spot on *Fox & Friends*.
Barack Obama had just delivered his well-received speech on
race relations in the wake of the Jeremiah Wright controversy, and the hosts, including Steve Doocy, spent a good part

of the show picking it apart. They invited Wallace to join in,
but he declined. "I told them that two hours of Obama bashing was enough," he recalls. Ailes was furious that Wallace
had criticized his colleagues on the air. "You shot inside the
tent," he said, and informed Wallace that he was a "jerk."
Wallace sent Ailes a letter of apology, and he hasn't forgotten
the lesson.

Ailes doesn't usually allow employees who leave the network for the competition to return. Fox News is a team, and
you don't leave your teammates to play for the other side. But
if you show the right kind of attitude, it can be done. Arthel
Neville proved that.

Neville joined Fox News as a correspondent and host in
1998. She is the daughter of Art Neville, the underappreciated member of the Neville Brothers, who is also a founder of
the Meters. Neville majored in journalism at the University of
Texas, became the first black on-air reporter at KVUE-TV in
Austin, and did a nationally syndicated TV show before coming to Fox.

Soon after arriving, Neville followed family tradition and
fell in love with a drummer. They moved to L.A. In 2002, she
got an offer to join CNN as the host of her own program, *Talk
Back Live with Arthel Neville* and as weekend coanchor with
Anderson Cooper. Before taking the job, she called Ailes.

"I did it out of respect," she says.

Ailes told her to go ahead.

In 2010, Neville returned with her husband to New York.
"When I called Roger about coming back to the network, the
first thing he said was, 'You still married to that drummer?'"
He was letting her know he remembered why she had left,
and that he had given her his blessing. She hadn't been disloyal and she was still welcome. "I feel very special about
that," she says.

Ailes has a knack for making his employees feel like friends, and his friends feel special. "Every time I meet with Roger he asks if I am all right and what do I need?" says Shep Smith. "When the meeting is over he says, 'I love you.' Roger is like a second dad. He's good to me. He changed my life. I wouldn't leave Roger any more than I would leave my brother. Roger doesn't just teach you how to be a better broadcaster; he teaches you how to be a better man."

Smith owes his career and his success to Ailes. A lot of people do.

Bob Beckel is a quintessential old-school political consultant, the kind of guy who worked hard during the day to make his candidates winners and harder at night, in the bars and clubs of America, to make himself a legend. A former football player and boxer, he could be a nasty drunk and he got into his share of brawls. He also developed a cocaine habit that was bigger than he was. The pinnacle of his career was managing Walter Mondale's presidential campaign; he borrowed "Where's the beef?" from a Wendy's ad and turned it into a Mondale slogan. But managing the Democratic catastrophe of 1984 wasn't really much of a credential. Beckel, who is funny and brash, was a better television performer than a political operator; he was scooped up as a talking head by various shows and caught on as a full-time commentator at CNN.

In 2002, Beckel was caught up in an extortion attempt by a prostitute. He says that he wasn't involved with her, and he had been part of a police sting. In any case, he gave her a check with his signature on it, a surpassingly naïve thing for a celebrity to do, even as a favor to the cops. The incident made headlines and CNN dropped him. "I went from making $750,000 a year to working at the Government Printing Office for thirteen bucks an hour, that's how screwed I was," he says.

Ailes saved him with a job offer.

"Roger and I go back," says Beckel. "We did the first *Politically Incorrect* with Bill Maher, on Comedy Central. We hit it off and stayed in touch. In the consulting business you make friends across the lines."

In 2004, Fox invited Beckel to come on and do a guest spot. "I didn't have a contract with CNN or anybody else, so I did it," he says. Ailes turned it into a one-year contract, and he's kept Beckel there ever since. In 2008, the gig became a full-time job, doing commentary on the Hannity show and, more recently, as the lone liberal member of the panel on *The Five*. "Roger cast that show as an ensemble—a femme fatale, a brainy woman, a leading man, a comedian, and a Falstaff. That's me. Falstaff."

Working at Fox was a difficult social adjustment. "You have to go pretty far to the left to be farther than I am," says Beckel. "I got shit from all my liberal friends. At one point, some of them actually staged an intervention."

It didn't snap him out of it. Beckel stayed at Fox, but he continued to be active in the Democratic Party. One night he was sitting in the bar of the Capital Hilton Hotel when two young men, delegates to the Young Democrats convention, came over and began berating him. "Roger Ailes is worse than fucking Hitler," one of them said.

"I lost it and put them both on the floor," says Beckel. "I was embarrassed about this. Shit, I did it sober."

The story got around Washington and made it to New York. Ailes sent Beckel a giant gift basket with a note: "Thank you for being loyal." When Ailes saw Beckel at Fox, he took him aside and gave him some advice handed down from Bob Ailes: "When you get into a fight, always go for the thumbs."

It's a good thing for Beckel that he earned Ailes's loyalty, because he has sometimes needed it. "When the show first started, I used the word 'bullshit' on the air four or five times. Roger took me aside and said, 'If you do that again, I'll put a five-second delay on the show.' I haven't done it again." What he did do, on the Hannity show, was tell a fellow panelist that she didn't "know what the fuck" she was talking about in a discussion about the efficacy of Head Start. Beckel said he didn't realize that he was on the air at the time. Another time, referring to commentator Roland Martin's suspension by CNN, he said, "The black dude got suspended at CNN for saying something on a tweeter, Twitter, twats, twits . . . sorry." Not many people would get away with saying "bullshit," "fuck," and "twat" on a family network and keep their jobs, but Ailes protected him. Not only that, he saved his life. At a festive lunch Ailes hosted to celebrate the success of *The Five*, Beckel got a shrimp stuck in his throat and began turning blue. Ailes jumped up and pounded him on the back until he could breathe again. "All those years in the bars. I got shot at, stabbed, been in two car wrecks, and Roger saved me from choking on a fucking shrimp."

"Everybody makes mistakes," Ailes says. "It's just human. If it is a pattern, or something done intentionally, that's different. But you don't fire anybody over a mistake." In 2009, on a Mediterranean cruise, Bill Sammon regaled his conservative audience with a tale of inside news making. During the 2008 campaign, Barack Obama had famously told 'Joe the Plumber,' an Ohio blue-collar voter, that there was nothing wrong with spreading the wealth around. "I have to admit that I went on TV on Fox News and publicly engaged in what I guess was some rather mischievous speculation about whether Barack Obama really advocated socialism, a premise that privately I found rather far-fetched," Sammon boasted. Fox critics learned about the speech and castigated Sammon for this obvious misuse of his position. There were rumblings in the Fox

Washington bureau that Sammon should be replaced as bureau chief. Ailes reprimanded Sammon but he also let it be known that he didn't consider it a firing offense. (Ailes himself made headlines, in 2012, when he said that comic Jon Stewart had once called himself a "socialist" in a barroom conversation. Ailes was derided by Stewart and others for what they portrayed as an exercise in right-wing witch hunting. Ailes, however, got the last laugh when a tape of Stewart describing himself to Larry King as "a socialist or an independent" turned up on the Internet.) Ailes watches out for his friends, but there are a lot of people out there who have his back, too. Some Friends of Roger are ideological fellow travelers or longtime employees. Others come from far outside what the public imagines his circle to be. People like MSNBC's Rachel Maddow, for example.

Roger and Rachel met at the White House Christmas party in 2009. Maddow was standing alone next to the tree when she saw Ailes break loose from a group of guests and walk in her direction. Maddow is the most provocative and successful cable host outside of Fox, but at that time she had been on the air for less than two years and she was still feeling her way. She also viewed Roger Ailes with considerable trepidation. But he introduced himself with an unanticipated compliment: "You're not good yet but you have the talent to be good," he said.

Maddow was intrigued. They struck up a conversation about television production. To her surprise, she found Ailes charming and friendly. The next day the *Huffington Post* ran a picture of the encounter, and Maddow sent Ailes a note. "I didn't want him to think that I agreed with the *Huffington Post*'s implication that this was a scandal," she says. Ailes sent a note back, assuring her that he had thought no such thing. It was the start of an off-the-record handwritten correspondence between them, mostly on the art of cable news. They didn't try to change each other's politics. "I think Roger's vision is wrong, but he's the most important Republican in the country," she says. "The party is like an old Ford Pinto, a hunk of junk, into which he has installed a jet engine."

"Rachel is good and she will get even better when she discovers that there are people on earth who don't share every one of her beliefs," says Ailes.

In March 2012, Maddow published her first book, *Drift: The Unmooring of American Military Power*. The jacket featured predictable blurbs by Frank Rich, Glenn Greenwald, and other progressives—and one from Roger Ailes: "*Drift* never makes the case that war might be necessary. America would be weakened dramatically if we had underreacted to 9/11. However, Rachel Maddow makes valid arguments that our country has been drifting toward questionable wars, draining our resources, without sufficient input and time. People who like Rachel will love the book. People who don't will get angry, but aggressive debate is good for America. *Drift* is a book worth reading."

The endorsement was heartfelt. "I don't reject a good idea just because it belongs to a liberal," he says. "Conservatives sometimes underestimate the value of diplomacy. And we need to discuss and seriously vet wars like Vietnam or Libya before plunging in. It's a point worth considering."

Ailes enjoyed the surprise he knew his endorsement of Maddow's book would generate. He also appreciated the opportunity to demonstrate his open-mindedness. He realized that praising Maddow would cause suspicion at MSNBC that he was planning to steal their brightest star. "I don't want to recruit her but they'll think I do," he told me with a grin. "Hell, they're paranoid over there." Maddow's book went to number one on the *New York Times* bestseller list, and although Ailes didn't put it there, the publicity surrounding his blurb helped publicize her book. Everybody came out ahead. Once again, Ailes had made the gift of friendship work for him.

Ailes had another surprise up his sleeve. Shortly after he endorsed Maddow's book, he announced that he had hired a new commentator: Santita Jackson, a Chicago radio talk show host who had recently lost her job. She was looking for a new gig, which her father happened to mention to Roger Ailes. Her father is Jesse Jackson.

"My father and Roger have known and respected one another for forty years," she told me. "My whole family is very supportive of my coming to Fox. Roger is a very authentic man, and he takes me as I am. It is an opportunity for both of us to broaden the conversation."

Quite a few bloggers and pundits on the right as well as in the African American community were disconcerted by the fact that Ailes hired Santita Jackson. Few people realized that Jesse Jackson, of all people, is a friend of "Brother Roger." Fewer know that Santita Jackson is one of Michelle Obama's closest friends: Jackson is a godmother to Malia Obama. Having her on board at Fox, in an election year, gives Ailes an interesting channel to the White House. It makes Fox more difficult to assault as a bastion of racism. It means that one of the nation's premier civil rights leaders owes him. And, as an extra bonus, it is sure to cause a little heartburn for Jackson's chief rival, Al Sharpton. After all, Sharpton has daughters, too.

CHAPTER TWELVE

MINORITY REPORT

Black History Month is celebrated by every television network, and Fox News is not an exception. Ailes commissioned a series of human-interest stories for the occasion, and he was here, in the conference room next to his office, to preview it. On hand were half a dozen members of the production team that put it together, all of them black or Hispanic.

The stories they screened were well done and unexceptional—a segment about a black opera singer who has overcome obstacles to achieve stardom, a piece about a polo team from inner-city Philadelphia, the profile of an adventurer/cancer patient who had ventured where no African American adventurer/cancer patient had traveled before. Ailes was especially interested in an interview with David Dinkins at Gracie Mansion, which Dinkins once occupied as New York City's first (and only) black mayor. These days Dinkins is a professor in the practice of public affairs at Columbia University. "Dave is a friend of mine," Ailes told the group. "I go up to Columbia

every fall and teach his class. I make sure that the kids up
there get a balanced education at least once a year." This was
greeted with mild laughter. Ailes punctuates his meetings
with stream-of-consciousness banter and throwaway lines.
When we first entered the room he introduced me as someone
writing a book about him and added, "A report by Zev will be
sent to your parents."

"I was up in Harlem at a church for Martin Luther King
Day," he told the group. "There was this cute eighty-five-year-
old lady sitting next to me, and when they sang 'We Shall
Overcome' she held my hand." I expected him to say that it
had been a moving moment of racial harmony. What he said
was, "Overcome, my ass. I think she was trying to hit on me."
There were more titters.

Racial identity politics are not Ailes's "thing." He belongs
to a generation that was raised in a time and place where
forward-thinking people accepted MLK's famous exhortation
to judge people by the content of their character, not the color
of their skin, as the gold standard for racial aspiration. In
Ailes's America, everyone would share Middle American,
middle-class values and blend into a single national culture.
He sees the celebration of racial differentness as balkanizing.
"Every month is something else," he said. "I'm waiting for
Lithuanian Midget Month. You know what? One of my rela-
tives actually *was* a Lithuanian midget." This got a real laugh.
Evidently it was the first time he had tried it out. "You are either American or you aren't," Ailes told me later. "Being Amer-
ican, living here is the only entitlement you need."

The next order of business was a report on the Ailes Apprentice Program, which is one of his proudest achievements.
Every year, half a dozen minority kids are selected and given
yearlong paid internships in an aspect of television news.
Ailes says that graduates are guaranteed a job. So far, there

are more than thirty former apprentices employed at Fox
News in some area of television journalism. Ailes started the
program as his version of private-sector affirmative action. "I
noticed that the kids who got internships here were mostly
white kids with contacts," he told me.

"Somebody knows somebody here, gets the kid in, and
then helps find him a mentor. Minority kids didn't have any
opportunities like that, so I decided I'd be their contact."

Ailes says that no other network has a similar program.
Neither do the other divisions of News Corp. "There are no
minorities in our film division, and they're a bunch of liberals. I don't wear pins or ribbons but I do give out jobs."

Sometimes these are dispensed on a whim. A few years ago,
Ailes noticed that the cleaning woman in his office was wearing a lot of makeup. He asked if she was going to a social event
after work. She admitted that she had been in a makeup room
and hadn't been able to resist giving herself the full treatment.

Ailes was intrigued. She told him she was a single mother
from North Africa whose dream from childhood was to be a
beautician. He decided a grand gesture was called for, and
sent her, at the network's expense, to a prestigious cosmetol-
ogy school, and then enrolled her as one of the first Ailes apprentices. Ailes didn't want me to think that this was mere
altruism. There was something in it for him, too. "I had seen
her around the office and noticed she was always in a good
mood," he told me. "That's critical for a makeup artist. They're
the last ones the talent encounters before going on the air. If
they are negative people, they can bring down the show."

Eric Deggans is the head of the media monitoring committee for the National Association of Black Journalists. His job
is to chart how black journalists are faring on television news
networks, and he is not a fan of Fox. He says he has never
heard of the Ailes Apprentice Program.

"He doesn't know because he doesn't want to know," says Ailes. "After all, it can't be true if I'm the one who's doing it."

Deggans says that Fox News reflects a "white gaze," which is undoubtedly true. It is also true for every other mainstream news organization. In 2000, Av Westin noted the problem in *Best Practices for Television Journalists: A Handbook for Reporters, Producers, Videographers, News Directors and Other Broadcast Professionals on How to Be Fair to the Public*, an authoritative guide published under the auspices of the Freedom Forum. Chapter 3 is titled "Bias," and it sets forth the situation across the spectrum of TV news. "The conventional wisdom among most assignment editors is that white viewers will tune out if blacks or Latinos are featured. . . . There is no question that a lack of racial sensitivity affects new judgment. It is a problem that goes to the heart of fair and balanced presentation of the news on television." The situation has changed since then. It has gotten worse, on TV and in print. According to a survey done by the American Society of News Editors, the number of minority journalists *declined* by 31.5 percent between 2001 and 2010, a finding Kathy Times, president of the National Association of Black Journalists, called "horrifying."

A Nielsen survey taken in 2010 reveals that blacks made up only 1.3 percent of the Fox audience (compared to 20 percent for both CNN and MSNBC). An overwhelming percentage of African Americans are Democrats and supporters of Barack Obama, and many tend to see Fox as the opposition. They aren't wrong, either. But in comparison with the industry standard, Ailes's minority employment record is pretty good. His very first hire at Fox was Lauren Green, now the network's religion correspondent. Wendell Goler is senior White House and foreign affairs correspondent. Brian Jones is number two at the Fox Business channel. Harris Faulkner,

Arthel Neville, and Charles Payne are all anchors or coan-
chors. There are others, as well, including a number of contributors and paid analysts.

To many African American journalists, simply going to
work at Fox News makes a black journalist inauthentic and,
in some sense, a collaborator with the enemy. "Fox may have
black people on the air, but that doesn't create diversity," insists Eric Deggans. Not surprisingly, this attitude irritates
black journalists who work there. "I got a lot of passionate
how-could-you's when I started at Fox," says Arthel Neville.
"But I never encountered racism there. Believe it or not, the
only incident I had with racial undertones was at CNN, when
an executive there said she wouldn't hire a woman named
Lakisha because she'd probably have an attitude. Nothing
like that has ever happened to me or anyone else, as far as I
know, at Fox News." Her sole complaint about Ailes is that he
hasn't provided a hairstylist who knows how to deal with her
hair. "The service at the network is basically for white women,"
she says. "I have to pay a hairdresser to do special chemical
treatments."

The idea that black reporters and commentators at Fox are
house Negroes on the Ailes plantation is infuriating to Jehmu
Greene. She first met Ailes at Harvard University in 2005,
where they were both participants in a panel discussion about
the junction of pop culture and politics. Greene was there as
the past president of Rock the Vote, the MTV initiative to
register young voters (she subsequently served as president of
the Women's Media Center, a nonprofit founded by Jane
Fonda and Gloria Steinem, and as a national director of the
Democratic Party's Project Vote, a group that worked closely
with other groups, including ACORN, to build the Obama
majority). She recalls the Harvard event, which was moder-
ated by Tom Brokaw, as "very white-centric. I was the only

person of color on the panel, and the only woman on the panel. I had come to talk about Rock the Vote, but nobody cared about it or what I had to say about it—except for Roger." She was surprised by their instant rapport. "I found him very authentic. In that world you don't meet a lot of authentic people. It felt good that night to know there was one person in the room who recognized my value."

As he did with Rachel Maddow, Ailes struck up an improbable friendship with Jehmu Greene. The Women's Media Center was trying to train young feminist activists in getting their message out, and Ailes volunteered to help. "Roger invited me to bring in a cadre of progressive women for a studio training session at Fox," she says. "Each one left that day with a professional reel. And to be clear, these were women who disagreed with him on 101 percent of the issues."

Greene had done a lot of talking head stints on MSNBC and CNN, but she was never offered a job. In 2010, Ailes hired her as a full-time analyst. Most important, she says, she is allowed to be herself.

"I'm a Democrat through and through. I have no desire to preach to the choir. At Fox I get a chance to talk to the movable middle."

It bothers Greene that her fellow progressives, white as well as black, regard Ailes as a bigot. "The left has a hard time coping with Roger's success," she told me. "They want cartoon characters. I know plenty of progressives who talk a good game on diversity, but it isn't reflected at all in how they operate. Roger walks the talk. America is very far from being a postracial society. I know that. But Fox News is postracial. This is the first time I've worked in an environment where I haven't felt barriers of race and gender."

It is easy to dismiss Greene, Neville, Juan Williams, and other black Ailes fans as self-interested. They are, after all, on

his payroll. But it is hard to argue that they haven't been allowed to express themselves on the network. In a Republican
candidate debate in South Carolina, Williams took on Newt
Gingrich's statement that blacks should demand "jobs, not
food stamps" and his suggestion that black kids bolster their
weak work ethic by doing part-time janitorial work, for pay, at
school. "Can't you see that this is viewed, at a minimum, as
insulting to all Americans, but particularly to black Americans?" asked Williams, who was booed by the mostly white,
conservative crowd. This is Fox's core viewership and there
were a lot of complaints, but Ailes loved the way Williams had
gone after Gingrich and the publicity it engendered. Here was
proof on a national stage that Fox would go after Republicans
aggressively; and besides, Ailes was getting sick of Newt's
bombastic campaign.

In April 2012, Elizabeth Warren, the Democratic candidate for the Senate in Massachusetts, got busted by her opponent, Scott Brown, for having claimed to be a Native
American. Her employer, Harvard, had listed her as a woman
of color (in fact, the only woman of color) on the faculty of the
law school. The story turned out to be not just bogus but ridiculous. Warren said she had 1/32 Cherokee blood, which,
even if true, wouldn't have qualified her for Cherokee tribal
registration. She couldn't even prove the 1/32nd claim. Worse,
she tried by pointing out that her aunt had once said of Warren's grandfather that he had "high cheekbones, like all Indi-
ans do."

The scandal was an Ailes trifecta. It underscored the ludi-
crous and self-serving nature of racial preferences based on
"blood." It made Harvard Law School look gullible (while un-
intentionally emphasizing how few women of color actually
teach there). And it could play a role in keeping the former
Ted Kennedy seat in the Senate in Republican hands.

Fox took up the story with vigor. In a panel discussion with Tucker Carlson and Megyn Kelly, Jehmu Greene came to Warren's defense. "You see Scott Brown really questioning her qualifications because he has to appeal to white, working-class voters who feel marginalized because of affirmative action," said Greene. "This smells real stank to women who do not like being called on their qualifications." She added that Tucker Carlson, a conservative contributor, was the sort of person this would appeal to—a "bow-tying white boy." At the end of the segment, Kelly apologized to the audience for a violation of the network's standards. Conservative cyberspace exploded with demands that Greene be banished for her racist remark. Typical was a column by Mychal Massie in WorldNetDaily. "Think of the level of betrayal Greene exhibited. She has been a Fox News contributor for a long time, and during all of that time, as she smugly sat arguing her leftist point of view, she secretly looked upon Carlson and every other white person with prejudice . . . if Fox News has any integrity, it should immediately and without apology fire Jehmu Greene."

Ailes didn't fire Jehmu Greene. On the contrary, he had every reason to be pleased with her. Mediaite, a website headed by former MSNBC general manager Dan Abrams, wrote that "perhaps Fox isn't as beholden to its decidedly right-leaning audience as many believe . . . the lack of punishment may also show that Fox has no interest in being the 'PC Police.'" Roger Ailes couldn't have made these points any better.

■ ■ ■

In *You Are the Message*, Roger Ailes had offered this advice:

A woman who acts like a man in the workplace is as silly as a man who acts like a woman in the workplace. Many women have felt, with some justification, that if they didn't toughen up and act macho, and be one of the boys, they would never get along. Women: Stay true to your identity. Whatever you do keep in mind that, as in all communications, your tone of voice, the expression in your eyes, the attitudes conveyed by your face and body will determine how others interpret your words. And above all keep your sense of humor and your sense of perspective.

In many ways, Ailes's views on gender have remained what they were when he wrote these words in 1989 (and, for that matter, what they were in 1969, and probably 1959). Ailes sometimes still refers to grown women as "girls." He doesn't like affirmative action for women any better than he does for ethnic or racial minorities. And, despite his old-fashioned notions of male gallantry, he is capable of shockingly bad manners in describing women who cross him. He infamously referred to Mary Matalin and Jane Wallace, the cohosts of a show on CNBC, as "girls who, if you went into a bar around seven, you wouldn't pay a lot of attention, but they get to be tens around closing time." When Paula Zahn left Fox for CNN, Ailes said he could have gotten better ratings with a "dead raccoon," and a spokesman for Fox compared her new show to putting a fresh coat of paint on an outhouse. To Ailes, such talk isn't a sign of disrespect or paternalism. It is a sign of equality. He talks about everybody that way, and if they can't take a joke (or an insult), well, that's their problem. Women, like men, are welcome to the club, but they have to be able to take a punch.

It also helps if they are beautiful. Ailes makes no apology for this. "Television is a visual medium," he says. "There's nothing wrong with having good-looking people on the screen." Some critics disagree. "When it comes to news readers, there is a look at Fox—blonde and attractive and somewhat interchangeable—that has gradually trickled down to the other networks," says Mark Danner. Jon Stewart and other comics have made a running joke of the "dumb blondes" of Fox News. "Sure, we have news actresses at Fox, just like the other cables do," says Brit Hume. "With a twenty-four-hour day, there are gaps to fill in, and they do news cut-ins or weekend jobs." There is, in fact, a high density of beauty queens and runway models at Fox, but looks can be deceiving. *Fox & Friends* host Gretchen Carlson is a former Miss America who plays the violin, matriculated at Stanford, and studied at Oxford. Shannon Bream, an anchor of *Fox News Headquarters*, is an attorney as well as a former Miss Virginia and Miss Florida. Kimberly Guilfoyle, one of the cohosts of *The Five*, modeled underwear for Victoria's Secret, but she was also a prosecutor in San Francisco and L.A. Arthel Neville came to New York as a model with a degree in journalism from the University of Texas at Austin. Martha MacCallum, the coanchor of *America's Newsroom*, worked for six years as a business correspondent at NBC and CNBC before joining Fox.

And not all of the beautiful women of Fox are blonde. Lauren Green was the third runner-up in the Miss America pageant in 1989, and is a graduate of the Medill School of Journalism at Northwestern University. She is also unmarried, a fact that prompted one of the more bizarre on-air exchanges in the history of television news. During an interview with Secretary of State Condoleezza Rice, Fox State Department correspondent James Rosen said, "I close with a gift for you. You met this person once, I believe, but you really ought to know each other because this woman, I think you'll have an interest in knowing her. She is one of our Fox News anchors in New York. Her name is Lauren Green. She is brilliant, she is beautiful, she is African American, she's single, and she's a concert pianist in her spare time."

"My goodness," Rice responded with diplomatic under-statement. Rosen proceeded to hand her a CD recorded by Green and informed Rice that his colleague was "going to want to hear from you." The exchange raised so many eye-brows that a mortified Green gave an interview to the *Minne-apolis Tribune* to clarify her status. "I am very straight," she said. "All Christian men, single and over thirty-five, can apply."

For all his political incorrectness, Ailes sees himself as a pioneer in the area of employing women. "I was the first to put a female on as host of a prime-time show," he told me. "That scared the hell out of the other cable networks." Greta Van Susteren, who now occupies the ten o'clock spot, is no-body's idea of a dumb blonde.

Megyn Kelly, on the other hand, is both blonde and brainy, and she has made good use of her glamour-girl image. She was discovered by Brit Hume, after his wife gave him a tape of Kelly (then Megyn Kendall) appearing on a local news show. "She looked stupendous and she had a really strong voice," says Hume. He sent the tape to Roger Ailes, who hired Kelly without even having an open job. She's a rising star: In addition to hosting her own show, she has appeared on presidential debates, and is scheduled to coanchor election night 2012. She is definitely being groomed for even bigger things.

Kelly has a history of playing with the "dumb blonde" ste-reotype. In 2010, she went on the Howard Stern show, where she unflappably bantered along with the ribald host. She also posed for a provocative photo spread and interview with *GQ*. In the interview, Kelly was asked about false rumors that she and Brit Hume were having an affair. She denied it, but Hume thought it was funny (and flattering). At his retirement dinner he called being linked to Kelly in the press "one of the greatest experiences of my life. It's not true. But it's not impossible!" It got a big laugh, especially from Kelly, who was worried that the story might be believed. Ailes, who learned about the GQ pictorial and the Stern appearance after the fact, thought they were too racy for a serious journalist and told her so. Kelly told Ailes that she didn't feel she had done anything wrong, but she also promised that it wouldn't happen again. But that's not to say that both Kelly and Ailes underestimate the appeal of attractive women on television.

Megyn Kelly's office at Fox looks like a boutique. She has closets full of clothing and a shoe rack displaying twenty-five pairs of hot-looking pumps. "It is a credit to Roger and his makeup and hairdressing team that the women at Fox have such an 'it' factor," she said. "The hairstylists, wardrobe people, and makeup artists here are better than at the other networks. They look to create a 'professional glam' and it works." Kelly is realistic enough to know that what she does—what all successful television journalists do—is a form of show business. "The whole day at Fox is cast by Roger," she says. "There are beautiful blondes, high school quarterbacks, brainiacs, and the entire spectrum." She is content to play her part because she sees the results. But she is not a femme fatale on the air. She was a practicing attorney for nine years, and she can be a tough, abrasive questioner. "Megyn doesn't back down for anyone," Ailes says. "She can even stand up to O'Reilly."

■ ■ ■

"I've been kicked out of every damn church I've ever belonged to," says Roger Ailes. It is a buccaneer's boast, meant to convey a hard-core irreverence. Ailes is not, by any means, a conventional born-again Christian of the Mike

Huckabee variety, let alone Pat Robertson or Jerry Falwell. He wouldn't use the word himself, but he is ecumenical. He donates considerable sums each year to a small Protestant church near his home in Garrison, although he is not on its membership rolls. He donates upward of 10 percent of his net income to charities, many of them religious, including an annual fifty grand to the Jewish Community Relations Council of New York and another fifty grand to Catholic charities. He told me he'd be glad to give to Muslim charities, too, "if they disarm."

Beth Ailes is a devout Catholic, and her husband often accompanies her to Sunday Mass at Our Lady of Loretto in Cold Spring; Beth occasionally plays the organ there. Their son is getting a Catholic education. Many of Ailes's closest associates are Roman Catholics, including legal consigliere Peter Johnson Jr.; his two senior deputies, Michael Clemente and Bill Shine (as well as his former head of news, John Moody); and Washington bureau chief Bill Sammon. Bill O'Reilly, Sean Hannity, anchorman Bill Hemmer, Bret Baier, Neil Cavuto, Doug Kennedy, and Megyn Kelly (to name but a few) are also practicing Catholics. For years, Fox had a permanent correspondent in Rome, Greg Burke, reporting on the Vatican (in June, Burke was appointed senior communications adviser to the Holy See). The network also employs Father Jonathan Morris as a full-fledged commentator on religious and church matters. Ailes told me he doesn't see anything unusual about this, but it is; very few national media organizations have such a concentration of openly devout religious believers of *any* denomination. Fox has the reputation of being something of a champion of the church. That has been notable in Fox coverage of the priest sex scandals of the past decade. "Roger isn't an apologist for the church," says Neil Cavuto, himself a former seminarian. "We cover the news."

Cavuto is right: Fox has covered the story, but less aggressively and with less hostility than many other major news organizations. Chris Cuomo thinks this is due to Ailes. "Maybe he doesn't light candles, but he also doesn't let people go on the air and beat up Catholics," Cuomo says.

In late May of 2012, forty-three Catholic archdioceses and organizations sued the federal government, on freedom-of-religion grounds, over the part of the Obama health plan that would require insurance companies to cover the cost of contraception for the employees of Catholic institutions and charities. A fight between the Catholic hierarchy and the White House is big news, especially in an election year, and Fox covered it that way. The other networks didn't. On the day the suits were filed, ABC and NBC evening news broadcasts ignored the story altogether. CBS gave it nineteen seconds. Bill O'Reilly, Sean Hannity, and Fox talking heads turned this seeming indifference into an illustration of the way in which the media attempt to minimize the importance of the official Catholic point of view.

■ ■ ■

Geraldo Rivera is Roger Ailes's favorite Latino journalist. He broke into the news business as a mouthpiece for a group every bit as radical and separatist as the New Black Panthers. In the late sixties, the Young Lords, a Chicago Puerto Rican street gang, transformed itself into a militant nationalist organization modeled on the (original) Black Panthers. A small delegation of New Yorkers traveled to Chicago and got permission from the Young Lords to open their own New York branch. In 1969, they made headlines with a series of public demonstrations, such as setting mountains of uncollected garbage on fire on Third Avenue and "liberating" property and redistributing it to the poor. At a time when the country was suffering from collective jitters caused by political assassinations and urban rioting, the general public found the Young Lords frightening, which was the point. The situation exploded when the group seized a Manhattan church and held it for eleven days. The publicity was enormous. Eventually 105 Young Lords were arrested. Their lawyer and advocate was a charismatic young Puerto Rican Jewish attorney, Geraldo Rivera.

Rivera was a natural media star, and he soon got job offers from clueless TV news directors desperate to find out what was going on inside a previously unknown community. He was hired by ABC, which billed him as "the first Latino reporting for a national network." But Rivera was more than a token. He did important exposés of life in the city, covered international conflicts with bravery and flair, and wound up as the senior producer and star correspondent of ABC's *20/20* newsmagazine.

Geraldo, who fashions himself "a barroom brawler, a guy who pushes back," made a lot of enemies at ABC with his flamboyant, ego-driven style of reporting. When Rivera publicly criticized Roone Arledge for spiking Sylvia Chase's story on the romantic relationship between Bobby Kennedy and Marilyn Monroe, Arledge fired him. He spent the next few years doing syndicated tabloid television shows, some of which made him a laughingstock. He did a talk show in which a skinhead punched him in the nose. His after-dark exploits made him a staple of New York gossip columns. He was making money, but for a serious journalist, which is how he saw himself, it was humiliating. He wanted professional rehabilitation, and in 1994, when Roger Ailes hired him at CNBC, he got it.

"Roger is my blood brother," Rivera told me. In 1996, when Ailes led his jailbreak from CNBC to Fox, Rivera didn't join.

He couldn't afford to; he had a $30 million contract. But after 9/11, when NBC declined to send him to the Middle East as a war correspondent, he turned to Ailes. "If you get out of your contract, come on over," Ailes told him. Rivera signed with Fox for about half of what he had been making and wound up where he wanted to be, a war correspondent in the middle of the fighting (and the center of the television screen).

Rivera is rich and famous and patriotic. But on social issues, he is an outspoken advocate for positions Ailes opposes. During the Occupy Wall Street encampment in 2011, Rivera did three live broadcasts that were clearly and proudly sympathetic to the demonstrators. And he is an outspoken supporter of amnesty for illegal aliens. Ailes kids him about this: "What are you, running for king of Mexico?" he asked after Rivera's book on immigration came out—but Rivera says he has never been told what stories to do or how to report them.

Despite their political differences, Ailes and Geraldo are close friends, and on Latino issues, he is a sounding board. During the Republican primary campaign, Rick Santorum traveled to San Juan to stump for Puerto Rican votes, claiming he had a good chance to win. The subject came up at an editorial meeting. Fox had political reporters covering the election, but Ailes wanted an expert opinion.

"What does Geraldo say?" he asked Bill Shine.

"Geraldo thinks Santorum is wrong," Shine said.

"Yeah, me too," said Ailes, dismissing Santorum's Puerto Rican strategy. And that was that.

There are other journalists at Fox News who come from Hispanic backgrounds. Juan Williams was born in Panama. Kimberly Guilfoyle of *The Five* is the daughter of an Irish father and a Puerto Rican mother. Correspondent Julie Banderas's mother is Colombian. They all allude to their ethnic

backgrounds from time to time, but they are American journalists who happen to have some Hispanic connection. In a
country in which Latinos and their children are now the largest single ethnic group (or collection of Spanish-speaking
subgroups), every media organization wants to reach and cul-
tivate that market.

Ailes's primary tool for this is Fox News Latino, a website
headed by Frankie Cortes, a young graduate of the apprentice
program. Cortes is clearly being groomed for an important
role in what will certainly be a bigger target area in the future. Ailes recently sent him on an Anti-Defamation League
junket to Israel. A report on that journey was the first item of
business at a lunch meeting Ailes chaired with the senior
staff of the website. Cortes said that he had been impressed
by the country, found the schedule hectic, and very much enjoyed the food (which, I can personally attest, is a step up
from the fare at Ailes's working lunches; this day the menu
was a choice of ham and processed cheese or tuna fish sand-
wich and potato chips). Ailes asked if ADL chief Abe Foxman
had been on the trip. Cortes said he hadn't been.

"Israel's in a tight spot right now, and this network stands
behind it all the way," Ailes said. This didn't come as a surprise to anyone at the meeting. There are two framed photo-
graphs in Ailes's office: One is of General George Patton; the
other shows him warmly shaking hands with Israeli prime
minister Benjamin Netanyahu. Hispanics, as a community,
are still making up their minds about the Middle East, and it
is important to Ailes to help them reach the "right" conclu-
sions.

Ailes asked for a report on the site, which was founded in
2010.

"It's really taking off," said Cortes. "We're getting three
million unique hits."

"Do you deal with the illegal immigration story or are you ignoring it?" asked Ailes. It was a management technique I saw him use repeatedly. There was no chance at all that Roger Ailes didn't know exactly how the website was reporting on the hottest issue of the day.

"We are, certainly," said Cortes.

"Where are people on this?" Ailes asked.

"We've got a poll that shows 70 percent of Latino voters are for Obama."

"What else does the poll show?" asked Ailes.

Cortes said that it revealed a high degree of optimism, especially when respondents were asked about their children's futures.

"That's because they haven't read the Obama health care plan yet," Ailes said. "You know, if I had to go to the army, I'd want to be with Latinos. They have a lot of medals." I was expecting him to order up a story on Hispanic military heroism, but his mind was on politics. "The main reason the Republican Party doesn't get the Latino vote is because it doesn't know how to talk to them," Ailes said. "Literally, we have to speak their language." This year, a new Spanish-language channel, MundoFox, began broadcasting two daily newscasts in Spanish (one for the East Coast, one for the West), anchored by Rolando Nichols of KWHY-TV, a Fox affiliate in Los Angeles.

Ailes has a heterodox position on illegal immigration, at least for a Republican in an election year. "Every country has to be able to enforce its borders. Otherwise there is no sovereignty. If I was president I'd do what's necessary, including putting Navy SEALs on the border with orders to shoot to kill drug dealers who are trying to infiltrate the country," he told me several months after this meeting. "Immigrants who have committed crimes should be rounded up and punished. But, at the same time, a lot of conservative views on immigration are

reactionary. Immigrants from Mexico are cultural conservatives and we should be encouraging them to come legally.
Texas and the other border states could be modern Ellis Is-
lands. Let 'em sign the register, make them hum a few bars of
'The Star-Spangled Banner,' and then welcome them to America."

Ailes is also happy to contemplate a deal that would allow
those here illegally to remain. "Any parent would do it for his
kids," he says. "Expulsion isn't a solution. I'm not big on
searching out people who are here without visas or papers.
Maybe make them do community service, or pay a fine of
some kind they can work off when they get on their feet. But
punishment? That's like punishing a seventeen-year-old girl
for having an abortion. It makes no sense."

For now, Ailes settled for marching orders. "Don't go soft
on the Republicans. They have to learn how to talk to Latinos. Is [Senator Marco] Rubio popular?" There was a brief
discussion of the question among the Hispanic journalists.
The consensus was, yes and no.

"I like Rubio," Ailes said. "But I don't know about as a vice
presidential candidate. He's a nice guy, and that role requires
kicking the crap out of your opponents. The first question
they [the candidate's vetting team] will ask him is, 'Can you
go after Obama?' And I'm not sure he can." He paused, thinking about vice presidents he had known.

"I have a soft spot for Joe Biden," he said. "I like him. But
he's dumb as an ashtray." He consulted his watch, popped a
last potato chip into his mouth, chewed thoughtfully, and
said, "This country will fail if we don't solve the immigrant
problem. America is a *culture*. We have to make sure everyone feels at home here. You are all trusted lieutenants. Just
remember, we are running a business here."

CHAPTER THIRTEEN

TAKING CARE OF BUSINESS

When I set out to write about Roger Ailes, one of the first calls I made was to Rupert Murdoch. I explained to his secretary that I was doing a book on Ailes and, while I of course understood that Mr. Murdoch is a busy man, I hoped he would find some time to talk to me about his partnership with Ailes. She assured me that she would pass the message along.

Fifteen minutes later, the phone rang. The secretary was on the line. "Mr. Murdoch will speak to you now," she said.

"Right now?"

"If that's convenient."

I had no questions for Murdoch. I hadn't even thought about any questions. I told that to the secretary and asked if we could schedule a time when I was better prepared.

"Just a moment, please," she said. The next voice I heard belonged to her boss. "I understand you want to talk to me about Roger," he said in the Australian accent that hasn't faded in the many years he has spent living in London and New York. "What would you like to know?"

"About you and Roger," I said. "Start anywhere."

"Roger Ailes has created an asset of enormous value," said Murdoch. He wasn't talking about value to the conservative movement, the Republican Party, the ideological balancing of American journalism, or any such nonsense. He was talking about money. In 2011, the division that Roger Ailes created from scratch accounted for more than one-third of the net income of News Corp, a company whose nearly countless holdings include such iconic companies as Twentieth Century Fox, the *Wall Street Journal*, the London *Times*, and Harper-Collins. "Roger surprised me with his executive ability," Murdoch said. "It's very unusual for such a creative guy to be a great businessman. Everyone thought we were nuts when we started out. And look where we are now."

Ailes's contribution to Murdoch's success galls his critics. "Ailes is clever, agile, swift, and a survivalist who can still— despite his advanced age and regal professional background— stomach taking orders and guff from another person," wrote Alexandra Kitty in her 2005 book, *Outfoxed: Rupert Murdoch's War on Journalism* (which is based on the documentary of the same name). "He is a media mogul's dream second-in-command: Someone who relishes his power as he relinquishes it. . . ."

This is a rather grim way of putting it, but there is no doubt that Murdoch is lucky to have Ailes, and he knows it. His gratitude is expressed the old-fashioned, capitalist way. In 2011, Ailes earned nearly $16 million, about half of it in performance bonuses. The following year he got a raise to roughly $21 million. "I'm not a manager at Wal-Mart who did a good job and got promoted to a bigger store," Ailes says. "I built the store."

"Rupert is not threatened by strong men around him," says Brit Hume. "He knows Roger is advancing his interests, and he's grateful because with Roger there he doesn't have to worry about one of his enterprises." Murdoch confirmed this. "Roger is paranoid about the opposition," he told me. "He or his wife is always watching the screen, keeping an eye on the competition. And he handles prima donnas very well. He runs as happy a division as we have at News Corp."

This is not a small matter. All is not well in the other divisions of News Corp, or in the Murdoch family. In 2005, his eldest son, Lachlan, lost a power struggle with Ailes over who would control News Corp television properties, and Lachlan departed for Australia. The *Wall Street Journal*, not yet owned by Murdoch, published a front-page story claiming that Ailes's performance as chairman of Fox Television had been disappointing and that he had "ruffled feathers" among fellow executives at News Corp. In response, Ailes and Murdoch gave a rare joint interview to the *Financial Times* in which Murdoch called the story "a hit job" and "absolute crap." He said that Lachlan's departure was sad, but the job he had sought, which would have put him over Ailes, was too big for the boy. "I admire him greatly but there is a difference between being number one in Australia and being number three [in the United States]," Murdoch said. Number three is Roger Ailes.

Murdoch's daughter Elisabeth is married to Matthew Freud, a powerful British public relations executive who disapproves of Fox News. "I am by no means alone within the family or the company in being ashamed and sickened by Roger Ailes's horrendous and sustained disregard of the journalistic standards that News Corporation, its founder, and every other global media business aspires to," he told the *New York Times* in 2010. A spokesman for Murdoch replied that his son-in-law had been speaking for himself, and that Murdoch was "proud of Roger Ailes and Fox News." Ailes mocked Freud in an interview in the *Los Angeles Times*, saying he couldn't pick the British adman out of a lineup and suggesting that he (a descendant of Sigmund Freud) "needed to see a psychiatrist."

Most recently, in London, Murdoch and his son James had been the subject of parliamentary questioning over allegations of bribery and phone hacking at a tabloid newspaper under the supervision of the division run by James. Subsequently, he was forced to step down as chairman and CEO of News Corp Europe and Asia, and as executive vice president of British Sky Broadcasting, a company in which News Corp was trying to gain a majority share. It was a painful episode for Rupert Murdoch. Meanwhile, Roger Ailes's money machine was smoothly turning out record profits.

Ailes and Murdoch are very respectful to each other. Ailes credits Murdoch with realizing that there was a niche audience ("half the country," as Charles Krauthammer, a Fox contributor, wryly put it) for a cable news network with a conservative perspective. Murdoch, for his part, assured me that he doesn't dictate editorial decisions. "I defer to Roger," he said. "I have ideas that Roger can accept or not. As long as things are going well . . ."

Murdoch often drops by Ailes's office to joke and gossip about politics. "Roger and I have a close personal friendship," he told me. Ailes agrees—up to a point.

"Does Rupert like me? I think so, but it doesn't matter. When I go up to the magic room in the sky every three months, if my numbers are right, I get to live. If not, I'm killed. Our relationship isn't about love, it's about arithmetic. Survival means hitting your numbers. I've met or exceeded mine in fifty-six straight quarters. The reason is, I treat Rupert's money like it is mine."

■ ■ ■

As a businessman, Ailes is self-taught. "I don't have a financial background," he told me. "I was terrible at math in school.
But I do have the ability to read financial sheets. I can look at
numbers and see aberrations and figure out what's going on."

In a meeting with senior ad salesmen Paul Rittenberg and
Jeremy Steinberg, the subject of political advertising arose.
The Romney primary campaign had just made a million-
dollar buy. "Call the Brain Room and find out what other
campaigns have money," Ailes instructed them. "Have you
spoken to Obama?"

"Nothing from them," Steinberg reported with a grin.

"We should send his people the Pew report that says we
have more independents than the other cable networks,"
Ailes said. "It would kill them to put ads on our air, but hell,
if they advertise on MSNBC all they'll get is Dennis Kucinich's family. By the way, when's the next Christmas
party?" Christmas was months away, and the segue seemed
to come out of nowhere, but I caught the two admen ex-
changing glances.

"I noticed I didn't get invited last year," Ailes said. It
sounded like rueful office sitcom humor, but Steinberg and
Rittenberg assured him that it had been a mistake and that
he would be on the list this Christmas.

Ailes nodded and went on to other matters, but as the
meeting was breaking up, he returned to the party. "Jeremy,
it's your ass if I don't get an invitation. And I want a head
count."

After they left, I asked Ailes why he gave a damn about
being invited to an office party. "They didn't invite me last
year because they didn't want me to know how many people
they've got working there," he said. "Here's the secret with

ad sales. Somebody is in first place. Somebody's number two. Then there's somebody number eighteen and she's really good-looking and doesn't do shit. I want to see who's there." Later he called his secretary and asked her to make sure he got an invitation and a copy of the guest list. They had promised him a head count, and they were his loyal lieutenants, but as an old client of his once said, "Trust, but verify."

In addition to Fox News, Ailes runs the Fox Broadcasting Company, thirty-five stations in twenty-six cities around the United States, including two in New York. His deputies are longtime colleagues. Jack Abernethy, the CEO of Fox Television Stations, came with Ailes from CNBC, where he had been chief financial officer. Dennis Swanson, president of station operations, has known Ailes since they worked together at TVN in the seventies. Since then, Swanson helped create *Monday Night Football* at ABC, gave Oprah Winfrey her first daytime talk show, and managed the NBC affiliate in New York City. They meet with Ailes periodically. One afternoon I joined them.

Ailes had the London phone-hacking scandal on his mind. "Do any of our local stations have investigative units?" he asked.

"Some," said Swanson. "Our Atlanta station broke the story about Herman Cain and his girlfriend."

Ailes's antennae went up. He wondered if the scoop might have come from someone close to the White House, to get Cain out of the race.

"The last thing the president wants is a black candidate going around saying he's against entitlements," he said.

"The woman was actually sad to out him," said Swanson. "But she was under pressure."

"She allegedly got $200,000 from somebody close to

Obama," said Ailes. He turned to me and said, "Write 'allegedly.'" (The story didn't pan out and Fox didn't report it.)

"Cain's shopping a new show," said Swanson.

"Nobody will touch him," Ailes predicted. "They won't
want a black man who is against entitlements." That settled,
he turned to the business at hand. "Where are the candidates
advertising?" he asked. "How much and in which markets?" It
was commercial information, but it would also give him a
read on how much money the candidates were actually raising. He asked about Target and Wal-Mart, and was told that
they had decided to advertise on the Big Three networks.
Ailes told them to work on the box-store chains, and they assured him that it was already being pursued.

"Car advertisements are up," said Abernethy. "Movies, not
so hot."

Ailes had recently seen and liked *Act of Valor*, a movie
about the Navy SEALs that was doing big business at the box
office.

"Most of the reviews were bad," Abernethy observed.

"Of course they were bad," Ailes said. "The reviewers are
all liberals."

Nobody disagreed.

Ailes wanted to talk about Saturday night. "What about
Regis Philbin?" he asked. Philbin had recently retired from
ABC's *Live! With Regis and Kelly* after a twenty-eight-season
run with multiple cohosts. "I've known Regis since 1963, and
he's still a hell of a talent. Maybe we could use him on Fox
News for an hour on Saturday nights, drive the ratings? Or
maybe do a syndicated show with him."

The meeting ended with a discussion of Sunday morning
soccer. Fox had recently acquired the rights to English Premier League football, which, because of the time difference,
ran on Sunday mornings. Stations around the country had

preempted Chris Wallace's interview program and moved it to a different time slot, making it hard to find. Not only that: Fox Sports wanted Brian Kilmeade, the cohost of *Fox & Friends*, who knows the game well, to take part in the broadcasts. Ailes didn't care for this one bit; he was afraid it was a case of incipient talent-nabbing by the sports division. "*Fox & Friends* is all about balance among the hosts, and I don't want to upset that," he said. "Tell them to find somebody else." Nobody was going to mess with Roger Ailes's winning combination for the sake of goddamn soccer.

Critics who chafe at Ailes's seemingly endless string of successes have taken heart from the struggles of Fox Business News. "It hasn't worked," Av Westin told me with unmistakable schadenfreude. "Roone Arledge knew how to fix his failures. You don't see that with Roger."

That is a premature judgment. When Fox Business first went on the air, in 2007, it averaged 6,300 viewers a day. It still runs far behind CNBC by as much as five to one, but it is doing better financially than is generally assumed. Ailes had a clause in his contract that called for a $3 million bonus if Fox Business broke even by 2012, and he collected a year early. "We're even," he told me. "Fox Business isn't costing Rupert a penny, and that's a pretty big asset to be sitting out there."

Still, breaking even isn't what Ailes does, especially when he is still trailing a network he once ran, and whose biggest star, Jim Cramer, he once fired. "We could spend $100 million on Fox Business News and change the game," he says. "I just have to convince Rupert. I think I can."

Part of the equation is talent. Ailes has been tinkering with the network for several years. In 2009, he jacked up morning ratings by hiring Don Imus, who had left his MSNBC television slot in disgrace after calling the black players on the Rutgers women's basketball team "nappy-headed hos." "He apologized and I felt he had paid his dues," says Ailes. The following year Ailes poached Gerri Willis from CNN to bolster the evening schedule. And in 2011, he signed Lou Dobbs, the erstwhile star of CNN's business news, whose vocal opposition to illegal immigration and clashes with the network's president, Rick Kaplan, cost him his job. Dobbs has since become FBN's most popular host. Ailes scored again when he picked up nineteen-time Emmy winner John Stossel, the libertarian former cohost of ABC's *20/20* who does double duty on Fox News. With the right talent on board, Ailes changed the entire prime-time roster in early 2012, dispensing with poorly performing shows by David Asman, and the controversial Andrew Napolitano, a high-profile, low-ratings supporter of Ron Paul.

But raising FBN's profile requires more than talent. It needs promotion. Ailes had his sights set on the recently vacated Charles Schwab space on the ground floor of the News Corp building, on the corner of Sixth Avenue and Forty-Seventh Street. Other divisions of News Corp were interested in laying hands on the spot, but Ailes intended to get it and use it as a showcase for FBN. On a sunny afternoon in early April, dressed in his customary black suit and accompanied by the network's chief engineer and a small retinue of aides, he set off on an exploratory foray.

The first stop was the current FBN studio, where Ailes was greeted with collegial handshakes by the crew. There were markers and obstacles on the floor, and a nervous young cameraman warned him to watch his step. "I've been in television studios for fifty years," Ailes said, and began firing off a barrage of questions. "Why are there no accordion lights here? How quickly can you turn around the set? How many shows are currently being shot here? How many could be? What is the actual height of the ceiling? What is the capacity of the backstage area?" He already knew the answers to these questions, but they would come up when he made his pitch for the new real estate. Ailes walked over to the huge windows facing Sixth Avenue. "What's the stop on this glass?"

".357 caliber," said the engineer.

"At what range?"

"Close up," the engineer said. Ailes nodded. You put a television show on street level, you had better be prepared for armed critics.

From the studio we went down to the ground floor. There was a TV screen in the elevator; a young woman was talking, although the volume was down too low to hear her. "Is she on our air?" Ailes asked.

"No. I think this is a spot for Fox International," an aide said.

"The direction is crap," said Ailes without emotion. "Lousy framing on the bottom of the screen and the camera angle is wrong. Check into it."

Ailes always has one eye on the screen. One day I walked into his private office and found him on the phone deep in conversation with the head of the Fox Television Stations group. "I'm watching channel five right now and there's something off with the shot," he said.

On the screen was a morning interview show with two hosts, a man and a woman, and a guest. The conversation didn't matter to Ailes; it was the picture. "You don't see our guy's smile," he said into the phone. "All you see is him from the side. His ear. Nobody wants to see an ear shot." There was a pause and then Ailes said, "There's a problem with the damn framing. And when the guy leans forward, he blocks the guest. Everybody's sitting on a three-quarter shot. People at home don't get a sense that anyone is talking to them. Get it fixed." He hung up and looked at me. "Television is painting the *Mona Lisa* and you have to do it every three seconds. Right now the head of the station group is calling the station director, who is about to call the executive producer of the show, who will"—he checked his watch—"be calling the line producer right about now and telling him, 'Ailes says it looks like shit. Change the fucking screen.' What the hell, I can't help it. I'm still a director."

We descended to the ground level and entered the cavernous Schwab space. Ailes clapped his hands to test the acoustics. "What is this, about twenty feet?" he asked, looking at the ceiling. "Eighteen," the engineer said.

"We could put two floors in here," said Ailes.

"Or lifts, so we could raise and lower floors," said the engineer.

"Let's not get too fancy," said Ailes. "You start raising and lowering the floor, somebody will get stuck halfway up. Let's not invent trouble."

The engineer nodded. It was the response he seemed to be anticipating. When it comes to technology, Ailes isn't enthusiastic. CNN had recently introduced a new graphic design with moving walls, which Ailes thought was foolish. "You've got Wolf Blitzer standing out there facing the camera, and suddenly the set moves and you're looking at his rear end. Wolf's a good journalist, but I doubt if the audience really wants to see some sixty-four-year-old short guy with his back to the camera. That's a production mistake whether the walls move or not."

Ailes isn't an early adopter when it comes to equipment, either.

"Let CNN buy the new stuff and test it out, and when the technology is right I'll come in like a ton of bricks," he says. "One of the laws of television is that the head of engineering always wants new stuff. You spend a million dollars on some innovation and it turns out that nobody in the department knows how to use the damn thing. So they need something else to make it work. It never stops. When I see that the Framistan is working, we'll get one. Hell, we'll get two. But in the meantime, let CNN waste their money." Framistan, it turns out, is a word Ailes loves. It became popular after it was used on an episode of *I Love Lucy*—it stands for unnecessary gear. "Framistans always need an additional Framistan. And this network isn't going to run in the red."

No, Framistans weren't what Ailes wanted. He was looking for a window display, where passersby in the heart of midtown Manhattan could see for themselves that the journalists of Fox Business were hard at work—and that they merited prime real estate. He needed a window and he needed a slogan. The next time I came by, he had both. A huge banner was draped over the old Schwab office. It read "Fox Business News—the Power to Prosper."

CHAPTER FOURTEEN

"THE MOST POWERFUL MAN IN AMERICA"

During the presidential campaign of 2008, candidate Barack Obama was upset by Fox News, which by then was in its sixth year of cable dominance. He was being treated deferentially (and, in some quarters, worshipfully) by most of the media, but getting roughed up on Fox, especially by Sean Hannity and Glenn Beck. A sit-down was arranged with Rupert Murdoch and Roger Ailes to get Fox's mind right.

Ailes recalls that the meeting took place in a private room at the Waldorf Astoria Hotel in Manhattan (White House spokesman Jay Carney declined to relate the president's version). Obama arrived with his aide, Robert Gibbs, who seated Ailes directly across from Obama, close enough for Ailes to feel the intention was to intimidate him. He didn't mind; in fact, he rather appreciated the stagecraft, one political professional to another.

After some pleasantries, Obama got to the point. He was concerned about the way he was being portrayed on Fox. Ailes responded that the news coverage thus far had been fair and balanced, and would continue to be. Obama said that his real issue wasn't the news; it was Sean Hannity, who had been battering him every night at nine (and on his radio show, which Fox doesn't own or control). Ailes didn't deny that Hannity was anti-Obama. He simply told the candidate not to worry about it. "Nobody who watches Sean's going to vote for you anyway," he said.

Obama then asked Ailes what his personal concerns might be. It is a politician's question that means: What can I do for *you?*

Ailes said he was mainly concerned about Obama's strength on national security issues. The candidate assured Ailes that he had nothing to worry about.

"Well, why are you going around talking about making cuts in weapons systems?" asked Ailes. "If you're going to cut, why not at least negotiate them and get something in return?"

Obama said that Ailes had been misinformed; he was not advocating unilateral cuts.

"He said this looking me right in the eyes," says Ailes. "He never dropped his gaze, which is the usual tell. It was as good a lie as anyone ever told me. I said, 'Senator, I just watched someone say exactly that on my computer screen before coming over here. Maybe it wasn't you, but it sure looked like you and sounded like you. I think it was you.'"

At that point, Gibbs stood and announced that the session was over. "I don't think he liked the meeting very much," says Ailes.

Relations between Ailes and the Obama administration were bad from the start, although in his first few months in office the White House focused most of its media fire on Rush Limbaugh. But under the surface there was considerable tension, and it came to the surface with the Van Jones affair.

Jones was the environmental activist appointed in 2009 by Obama to the newly created position of Special Adviser for Green Jobs, Enterprise, and Innovation at the White House Council on Environmental Quality. Jones wasn't well known, but he seemed to be an attractive, well-qualified Yale lawyer whom *Time* magazine had named one of its "heroes of the environment." But Fox, led by Glenn Beck, took a closer look at his background, which included youthful involvement in a radical organization, Standing Together to Organize a Revolutionary Movement (STORM) and, more recently, advocacy for convicted murderer—and alleged political prisoner—Mumia Abu-Jamal. Beck also claimed that Jones had signed a petition suggesting that the Bush administration may have been complicit in the attacks on September 11, 2001 (a claim he waffled on and then denied). And Fox reported that Jones had referred to congressional Republicans as "assholes," for which he apologized. All this was too much turbulence for the White House. Jones was allowed to resign, and spokesman Robert Gibbs remarked coldly that President Obama did not endorse Jones's statements but "thanked him for his service."

Roger Ailes and Van Jones had tangled before. In 2007, Fox and the Congressional Black Caucus announced that they were going to cosponsor two debates, one Republican, one Democratic, in the 2008 presidential primaries. This wasn't unprecedented; Fox had cosponsored a debate with the CBC in 2004, in Detroit. The Nevada Democratic Party had recently agreed to hold a debate on Fox. Grassroots reaction had forced the Nevadans to cancel, though, and there was pressure for the CBC to do the same. The effort was led by a group called ColorOfChange.org, which accused Fox News of racism and called the CBC's decision to partner with it "shamefully out of step with most black voters." Van Jones was the cofounder of the group.

After Obama won the nomination, ColorOfChange.org, along with MoveOn.org and other progressive groups, launched a nationwide petition drive aimed at branding Fox a racist network. The petitions, which had 620,000 signatures, were delivered to Fox headquarters.

A lot of people at the White House thought that Obama had let Jones go too easily. "He was very close to Michelle Obama in particular," says Bob Beckel. "She blamed Fox for getting him fired. After that, a lot of Democrats grew leery of even coming on Fox."

Not long after the Jones episode, the White House press office set up five-minute interviews for each of the networks with Kenneth Feinberg, the "pay czar." Fox was excluded. It was the first time anyone could recall that an administration had banned a network from the press pool. The Washington bureau contacted Ailes, who went to work.

Ailes had been expecting something like this, and he was prepared. "Roger doesn't believe in blind rage," says Woody Fraser. "He believes that if you have to fight, you build for it. When this happened, he was ready." Ailes contacted the heads of the other networks, reminded them that they were all equal partners in the costs of the pool, and that what happened to Fox could happen to them, too. He also mentioned the possibility that barring Fox could be a government violation of press freedom. The networks got the message; nobody wanted to be on the wrong side of the First Amendment. Fox got its interview with Feinberg.

About this time, the White House spokesman Gibbs began saying that Fox wasn't a real news organization. At a briefing, ABC correspondent Jake Tapper asked him how Fox differed from the other networks. "You and I should watch sometime around nine o'clock tonight or five this afternoon," Gibbs replied. Those were the times the Glenn Beck and Hannity shows aired. "I'm not talking about [Fox] opinion programming, or issues you have with certain reports," said Tapper. "I'm talking about saying that thousands of individuals who work for a media organization do not work for a news organization. Why is that appropriate for the White House to say?"

"That is our opinion," Gibbs replied.

The White House was not winning this particular battle. The Democratic base hated Fox, of course; bashing it played well on campus and in the big blue states and cities. But Fox had millions of viewers, and surveys showed that a great many were liberals or moderates. At the height of the crisis, Ailes met with David Axelrod in New York.

The meeting was cordial but it didn't end the tension. Anita Dunn, the White House communications director, went on CNN's *Reliable Sources* and revived the "Fox isn't a news organization" meme. "I think what is fair to say about Fox, and certainly the way we view it, is that it really is more of a wing of the Republican Party," she told host Howard Kurtz. She added that Fox viewers during the 2008 campaign, which took place on the backdrop of the financial collapse, would have concluded that "the biggest stories and the biggest threats facing America were a guy named Bill Ayers and something called ACORN."

Dunn was mistaken. Fox News, like all the other news networks, reported incessantly on the financial meltdown and its consequences. No Fox viewer could have missed it. Fox talk show hosts, especially Beck and Hannity, *did* focus heavily on Ayers, ACORN, and Obama's pastor, Jeremiah Wright, and to an extent that was partisanship (Hannity is a self-declared Republican who refers to the GOP as "we"). But Fox also had a very valid journalistic reason to pursue these stories. The mainstream media (abetted by the Republican candidate) barely reported on Ayers, Wright, and ACORN at all. Unburdened by such inhibitions, Fox had almost daily scoops on the background and associations of the little-known Obama. Fox viewers knew *more*, not less, than the viewers of other television news (or, for that matter, the readers of the major newspapers).

In the midst of the face-off between Fox and the White House, Roger Ailes made a rare television appearance on ABC's Sunday show, *This Week*. Barbara Walters was the substitute host and she wanted a ratings smash, so she brought on Ailes to spar with Arianna Huffington and Paul Krugman. Ailes very seldom appears on TV, and the show competed directly with Fox News' own interview program, but a friend is a friend. Walters was after fireworks and Ailes provided them. Arianna Huffington rebuked Ailes for allowing Glenn Beck to engage in uncivil and extreme language on his show. Ailes said that Beck had apologized, but that he, Ailes, didn't want to police language on the air (in fact, he was already figuring out how to get rid of Beck, but he wasn't about to say so on ABC). Huffington pressed her point.

"It's not about the word police," she said. "It's about something deeper . . . the paranoid style [used by Beck] is dangerous when there is real pain out there."

Ailes's candidates never come to a debate unprepared, and neither does he. "I agree with you [about the need for civility]," he said. "I read something on your blog that said I looked like J. Edgar Hoover, I had a face like a fist, and I was essentially a malignant tumor— . . ."

"That was never by anybody that we had—" Huffington protested.

"But then it really went nasty, and I thought, Gee, maybe Arianna ought to cut this out. . . ."

Ailes and Krugman, a Nobel laureate in economics, got into it over the still-pending health care legislation. Krugman charged that Fox had intentionally obscured the meaning of the bill. Ailes replied that the bill was thousands of pages long. Krugman said that legislation is always long. Ailes pointed out that the Constitution is considerably shorter. Looking back on the exchange, Ailes is dismissive. "All Krugman wants to do is give away money. That's his answer to everything. He's a dope but nobody wants to say it because he's won awards."

The topic that most interested Walters was the Fox-Obama dustup. "You have had your own back-and-forth with the White House," she said to Ailes. "They were not very happy with you, banned you for a while. Have you kissed and made up? Is it hunky-dory?"

"Well, they tried to ban us," Ailes replied. "They wanted to break the pool but the other networks stepped up and protected Fox on it, because it was . . . interference with a contractual relationship and sort of tramping around on the Constitution. . . ."

"But now you're okay?"

"We're fine. I mean, we were—it was not as bad as it was played, and things are not as great as they should be, but we have a good dialogue. And I saw the president and his wife at the media Christmas party. They were very gracious, very nice, both of them. And we have a dialogue every day with them."

Ailes didn't originally want to go to the Christmas party: Getting around is hard for him, and he's already been to the White House. But it was an opportunity to introduce his son to the president, and so he and Zac went to DC. They stayed at the Jefferson Hotel because it has short corridors, and ate from room service.

At the party, when Ailes reached Obama in the receiving line, the president said, "Here comes the most powerful man in America"—a joking but pointed reference to an article that had recently dubbed the Fox chief with that title. Ailes leaned in to the much taller Obama and said, "Don't believe that bullshit, Mr. President. I started that rumor myself."

Ailes was never concerned that the White House would actually close Fox out. And there was value to him, with his own base, in playing up the drama. Meanwhile, at his direction, the Fox bureau in Washington was finding a modus vivendi with the White House. "Even in the darkest times, when White House officials said outrageous things about our news product, we still had communications with the president's staff," says Bret Baier, the anchor of Fox News' 6:00 p.m. *Special Report*, who replaced Brit Hume. "Sometimes it was surreal. Anita Dunn would be outside telling reporters that Fox News is the media arm of the GOP while we were inside the White House working with people in the administration. We understood at the time that what Dunn and some others were doing was putting on a political show."

As Ailes predicted he would, Obama caved. He needed the Fox audience. Three days before the health care bill passed Congress, he gave Baier an interview. It was contentious, but it didn't lead to a new boycott. "Obama understands the power of Fox in an election year," says Baier. "We still don't have the kind of access to the president that others have—Chris Wallace and I have each interviewed him once, and O'Reilly has had him on twice. I think he's been interviewed on NBC something like fifteen times. But we're not blacklisted anymore."

By the time Ed Henry joined Fox News in the summer of 2011 as senior White House correspondent, hostilities between Fox and the Obama administration were in a lull. Henry had been the senior White House correspondent at CNN, and he understood the cease-fire would be temporary. The new job would be a combat assignment.

Henry had his doubts about joining Fox. CNN was a sinking ship—everyone there knew it. But he was concerned about being stigmatized as a right-wing propagandist. The concern was assuaged when he met Supreme Court justice Stephen Breyer at a Washington dinner and the liberal jurist told him that the news show he watches every night is *Special Report* because he finds the reporting so straight.

But Henry had another concern. The job offer had come from Michael Clemente. He had never actually met Roger Ailes. "All I really knew about Roger was the caricature of him as a right-wing ogre," he says. But he trusted Clemente and he decided to take the job.

"After the deal was done, I took the train up to New York to meet Ailes," he recalls. "There was a sense of mystery around him, which I felt while I was in his waiting room. When I finally walked in, he looked at me and said, 'This company was doing great and then we hired you, and now it's all fucked up.'" Then he burst out laughing. Henry got the full Ailes treatment—the profane banter, the cynical asides, and the camaraderie that goes with joining the team. He found himself wishing he had a camera to record it.

Finally Henry asked Ailes why he had been hired.

"I could see that you are a fair reporter," Ailes said. "You're earnest, and that comes across. This is a big beat and I need someone credible. The first day you go on the air for us, there's going to be a bull's-eye on your ass. You're going to be a target."

Ailes was right. At his first White House press briefing, presidential spokesman Jay Carney accused Henry of parroting Republican talking points. "He was testing me," said Henry, and it gave Henry a chance to test Ailes. "I've worked at other places where if you mix it up with a White House spokesman, the network's first instinct might be to appoint a task force to look into your behavior instead of backing you up."

Henry's apprehension grew when he got a message from Michael Clemente telling him to call headquarters. "I thought I might be screwed," he says. Clemente, speaking as always for Ailes, assured Henry that Fox wouldn't stand for Carney's bullying. Henry was charmed. "It wasn't the usual half-assed 'Maybe you went too far.' This was, 'We stand behind our guy.'"

A few weeks later, at a press conference, the president himself threw a brushback pitch. Henry asked about assertions by Mitt Romney that Obama was weak on Iran. It was a fair question in an election year, one that invited a rebuttal by Obama. Instead, the president said, "I didn't know you are the spokesperson for Mitt Romney." This time, Henry took the jibe in stride. "I'm supposed to ask hard questions. If it were a Republican president, I'm sure Roger would expect me to do the same thing. Eventually New York, L.A., and Washington, DC, will start to catch on to what the rest of the country already knows: There are a lot of strong, honest reporters at Fox."

In February 2012, Media Matters put out a book of Ailes's horribles, *The Fox Effect: How Roger Ailes Turned a Network into a Propaganda Machine*. The book itself didn't concern Ailes much, although he saw to it that friendly websites and some Fox commentators reminded America that the coauthor, David Brock, the head of Media Matters, does not exactly have a sterling reputation for honesty, and that the organization, which was founded with the "help and support" of the obviously partisan Hillary Clinton, is a political group that enjoys a charitable tax status. What really annoyed Ailes was that Senator Harry Reid went to the launch party in Washington and praised the book publicly. "We already know that Anita Dunn and Valerie Jarrett were coordinating the Media Matters war on Fox News, and now here's the majority leader of the Senate joining in. Two branches of government collaborating to shut down a news organization. What about the First Amendment? This is plain unconstitutional."

Media Matters and its right-wing opposite number, Media Research Center, are not, and don't pretend to be, objective or even open-minded analysts. They are partisan players, and their role is to find every possible way to discredit the opposition. This can be useful; there are enough mistakes in the media (and in the book-writing business) to keep armies of Washington-based nitpickers gainfully employed.

For Media Matters, Roger Ailes is one of the two Great Satans (Rush Limbaugh is the other). Every mistake or misstatement on Fox, which broadcasts 168 hours a week, is a premeditated lie. Every news story is an exercise in bias. Fox personnel are nothing but stooges in Roger Ailes's propaganda machine. People who watch Fox News are morons, either by birth or as a result of exposure to the network.

Media Matters is constantly on the lookout for scientific-sounding support for its ideology. It thought it had found some in a study by the University of Maryland, published in 2010, that purported to find that Fox viewers were the most misinformed audience of any network. This was so exciting that David Brock led his book with it, and Media Matters disseminated the findings widely. Eventually it made its way to Jon Stewart. Stewart, in turn, appeared on Chris Wallace's Sunday morning interview show. The invitation was a tribute to Stewart's influence as a satirist (and, not incidentally, a refutation of the idea that Fox doesn't allow its critics on the air).

Stewart and Wallace argued back and forth about the merits of the network, and Stewart closed the deal with hard evidence. "Who are the most consistently uninformed viewers?" he asked rhetorically. "Fox News viewers, consistently, every poll." Wallace didn't argue. He probably didn't know what Stewart was talking about. Neither did Stewart. PolitiFact .com, which belongs to the liberal *Tampa Bay Times*, pointed out what everyone who hadn't bought the Media Matters hype already knew: The Maryland study did not demonstrate that Fox viewers were less or more informed than anyone else. Stewart, who suffers from an exceptional degree of intellectual honesty, publicly apologized.*

A lot of the Media Matters oeuvre amounts to stating the obvious in terms of the scandalous. Fox reporting on the war in Iraq was more positive than that of other networks! Fox reporting on the Obama health care legislation was more negative! This doesn't demonstrate that Fox reporting on these and other subjects is more or less correct, merely that it differs from what Media Matters regards as truth as measured

---

* At the end of September 2012, Pew, a disinterested and respected organization, published its own survey of audience general knowledge based on four relatively easy questions about current events. MSNBC led the cable networks with 21 percent of viewers who scored four out of four. Fox and CNN finished in a virtual tie—CNN, 17 percent, and Fox, 16 percent. Both beat the audience of network news (15 percent).

Among viewers who scored three or more correct answers, Fox trailed MSNBC by 6 percent but led CNN by 4 percent and network news by 3 percent.

As for specific shows, Stewart's *Daily* viewers outpaced O'Reilly's *Factor* audience in perfect scores (32 percent to 26 percent); the two shows had similar numbers for at least three correct answers (61 percent to 59 percent); but twice as many Stewart viewers got zero correct (10 percent to 5 percent for O'Reilly).

Surveys like this are fun, but what they measure is unclear. After all, most people have more than one source of general political information.

by the distance between any story and Democratic Party talking points.

Roger Ailes often boasts that Fox hasn't had to take down a story in fifteen years. Lately he has amended that: He says he means a major story, like Dan Rather's career-ending, unsupportable allegations that George W. Bush dodged his Texas Air National Guard duty; CNN's bogus Tailwind scandal; NBC's rigged "exploding GM truck" affair, or that network's subsequent firing of three employees for doctoring a 9-1-1 tape to make it sound like George Zimmerman shot and killed Trayvon Martin for racist reasons (which may or may not be the case). But Fox has made plenty of mistakes. Shep Smith once announced the death of a pope a full day before the pontiff stopped breathing. On another occasion, Smith got his tongue twisted in an embarrassing way, reporting that while Jennifer Lopez considers herself a neighborhood girl at heart, her actual neighbors are "more likely to give her a curb job than a blow job . . . rather, 'block party.'" In both cases he apologized; in the latter, Ailes thought it was funny. And during the war in Iraq, Fox hired a bogus lieutenant colonel as a military analyst. Upon closer investigation, his entire army résumé consisted of six weeks of basic training.

A more serious incident took place in the early days of the Afghanistan war. On December 6, 2001, Geraldo Rivera reported on an incident in which "our men" had been killed by friendly fire. Six days later, David Folkenflik reported in the *Baltimore Sun* that Rivera had not been at the battleground but hundreds of miles away. Rivera explained that he had confused the friendly fire incident with a similar one. Ailes, as usual, stood by his man: Fox issued a terse statement on December 26, acknowledging that its correspondent had made an "honest mistake," since corrected. The story might have ended there, but Rivera demanded an apology from

Folkenflik for questioning his honesty. Rivera grew more irate when the Center for Media and Public Affairs awarded Folkenflik a prize for investigative reporting. Rivera still insists that he was guilty of nothing more than reporting in the midst of the fog of war. Folkenflik, now a media reporter for NPR, not only rejects this explanation but has publicly chided Ailes for failing to issue an on-air retraction.

None of these errors were partisan. But that can't be said for three on-air incidents that took place during the 2008 primary campaign. In one, E. D. Hill, host of the daytime *America's Pulse*, wondered aloud if the greeting candidate Obama shared with his wife was actually "a terrorist fist jab." Hill apologized the next day on the air. Within a week Fox canceled her show and her contract wasn't renewed. She wound up as an anchor and host on CNN. Around the same time, Fox reported a story taken from a conservative website that Hillary Clinton's campaign was circulating rumors that Obama had been educated in Islamic schools in Indonesia. The story was false, and John Moody sent out a curt note to the staff reminding them that merely appearing on a website did not qualify a story as credible. "We violated one of our cardinal policies," Moody told me. "We went on the air without knowing what we were talking about."

News analyst Liz Trotta made it a trifecta. Discussing a remark by Hillary Clinton about the assassination of Bobby Kennedy, she said, "Now we have what some are reading as a suggestion that somebody knock off Osama, uh, Obama. Well, both if we could." She apologized the next day for what she called a "lame attempt at humor," adding that it was a "very colorful political season, and many of us are making mistakes and saying things that we wish that we hadn't said." True, but the mistakes were all insinuations that Obama was connected to terrorism, Islamic radicalism, or Al Qaeda.

There were other misfires. In 2009, Sean Hannity showed footage of a crowd at a Michele Bachmann rally against Obamacare; it turned out to be video from a much larger rally held two months earlier. Hannity apologized the next day after he was busted by Jon Stewart. A week later, Gregg Jarrett reported huge crowds at a Sarah Palin book signing, with what turned out to be video from a 2008 campaign rally. Fox again apologized for the mistake the next day.

In March 2010, Shirley Sherrod, the Georgia state director of rural development for the federal Department of Agriculture, gave a speech at a chapter of the NAACP. In it she told the story of a white farmer who had appealed to her office for help to save some land. Her first reaction, she told her audience, was unsympathetic. She recalled the persecution of her family in the Jim Crow South and felt gratified that the shoe was now on the other foot.

The speech was recorded. Andrew Breitbart got a copy of it and shopped it around. Various websites, including Fox News, picked it up, and the story caused a furor. Sherrod was contacted by her bosses in Washington and forced to resign. The head of the NAACP, Benjamin Jealous, denounced her. Bill O'Reilly took up the case as a clear example of racial discrimination by an Obama administration official.

But, it turned out, the story Sherrod had told her audience came with a happy ending. She overcame her own prejudice, helped the white farmer, and learned a valuable lesson about fairness and tolerance. That part got left out of the video. The NAACP backtracked, exonerating Sherrod and condemning the deception. President Obama personally called Sherrod and let her know he was sorry for the way the Department of Agriculture had responded. And, on *The Factor*, Bill O'Reilly made his own mea culpa. "I owe Ms. Sherrod an apology for not doing my homework, for not putting her remarks into the proper context," he said.

"The Shirley Sherrod thing was a mistake," says Michael Clemente. "We went to air with it too early and it wasn't checked properly. My job is to make sure that something like that never happens again."

■ ■ ■

In the fall of 2011, Roger Ailes told journalist Howard Kurtz that he was turning down the partisan heat at the network. Ailes didn't say so, but he had already decided that, in the interest of a more moderate tone, he would have to get rid of Glenn Beck.

Beck came to Fox from CNN in 2009, and turned five o'clock—a perennially weak hour on the Fox schedule—into a bonanza. Beck contained multitudes—nerdy professor, slapstick comic, born-again preacher, shock jock, weepy recovering addict, man of destiny—and they all fought for airtime with chaotic results. Some of his colleagues at Fox considered him insane. But it was hard to argue with success. Beck was the biggest thing on the air at five o'clock, and five leads into the six o'clock news and then into prime time. For a while, he was worth the aggravation.

Beck had a way of settling on odd subjects, such as the villainy of Woodrow Wilson, and riding them for days. He compared victims of a mass murder at a camp near Oslo, run by the Workers' Youth League, to the Hitler Youth. He did a three-part series on George Soros, who, as a fourteen-year-old Jewish boy in occupied Hungary, had helped a Nazi seize Jewish property to protect his own life. Beck's source was Mr. Soros himself, who told the story in a *60 Minutes* interview with Steve Kroft, adding that he felt no guilt about it and that if he hadn't done it, someone else would. The ADL's Abe Foxman is-

sued a statement denouncing Beck's description as inappropri-
ate and offensive. "For a political commentator or entertainer
to have the audacity to say—inaccurately—that there's a Jewish boy sending Jews to death camps, as part of a broader assault on Mr. Soros, that's horrific." There was jubilation on the
left—not usually a Foxman fan club—for this condemnation,
but Beck responded by displaying a letter he had only recently
received from Foxman thanking him for being "a friend of the
Jewish people and a friend of Israel." Foxman subsequently explained that Beck was no anti-Semite, he was simply not aware
of the nuances and sensitivities at play.

The following Holocaust Remembrance Day, a group of
four hundred rabbis published an open letter in the *Wall
Street Journal* asking its proprietor, Rupert Murdoch, to sanc-
tion Ailes and Beck for the use of the word "Nazi" and other
Holocaust imagery. Ailes dismissed them as a bunch of political rabbis—a not unreasonable characterization of the orga-
nizers of the letter, the left-wing Jewish Funds for Justice.

"Roger's politics are less crazy than everybody thinks they
are," says Rick Kaplan. "When something goes off, he deals
with it. That's why he replaced the five o'clock show."

The final straw was the mass rally Beck staged at the Lincoln Memorial in Washington. Beck was already despised by
many blacks for speculating that Obama hated white people.
Convening a mass gathering at the site of Martin Luther
King's "I Have a Dream" speech—and featuring King's niece,
the Reverend Alveda King, delivering a conservative "I have a
dream" message of her own—was infuriating to many viewers. Ailes didn't like it much, either. When Al Sharpton called
him to complain, Sharpton was surprised to hear Ailes say he
would "take care" of it.

Ailes's method was patience and diplomacy. "To be fair,
Glenn showed signs of wanting to leave," he said. "He felt re-

stricted here. Sometimes he seemed too busy to concentrate on the show. And his emulating Martin Luther King was over the top."

Not only that: An advertising boycott organized by Color OfChange.org hurt revenues, and Beck's ratings declined after his march on Washington. Ailes spent months making him see that it would be in their mutual interest for him to leave Fox. "I could have done it in a harder way, but I didn't want to give MoveOn and Media Matters the satisfaction," he told me.

In April 2011, Beck announced he would be leaving Fox to start an Internet channel, Glenn Beck TV. As a face-saving move, it was announced that he would be cooperating with Fox to produce television and digital properties, although none have yet been undertaken. Ailes replaced the *Glenn Beck* show with *The Five*, whose ratings surprised everyone by approximating Beck's, and left the five o'clock hour firmly in the hands of Fox News. At the same time, Ailes could plausibly say that he had moved Fox safely away from the fringe. As for Beck, *Forbes* magazine reported that in 2011, he earned $80 million—more than any other political celebrity and much more than he had earned at Fox. Ailes was right again: Everybody came out ahead.

CHAPTER FIFTEEN

GOING TO CAROLINA

On a cloudless Thursday morning in mid-April, I met Roger Ailes, accompanied by his spokesman, Brian Lewis, and his security guard, Jimmy Gildea—the retired NYPD detective—at the airport in Teterboro, New Jersey. We were bound for the University of North Carolina at Chapel Hill, where Ailes was scheduled to address a crowd of journalism students. Ailes rarely makes public appearances. This one had been arranged long in advance, as a favor to a former colleague of one of Ailes's aides, but it was taking place when Ailes was in the center of two controversies.

Two days earlier, the gossip website Gawker had broken the news that there was a mole at Fox, documenting the claim by posting some innocuous off-camera banter between Sean Hannity and Mitt Romney. The mole wrote that he had been working at Fox for years but despised the place and now intended to tell all. The media jumped on the story; Fox News is regarded as one of the most leak-proof institutions in America. Finally the secretive Ailes was going to get his (presumably filthy) laundry aired in public.

Ailes knew better. "I'm the mole," he joked to a *New York Times* reporter at a party the night before the Carolina trip. By then, Ailes was aware that the mole had been found— Joseph Muto. He was caught on a hunch. The previous year, Beth Ailes had allowed the editor of the *Putnam County News and Recorder*, Joseph Lindsley, to resign after suspecting him of undercutting her with the staff and leaking information to hostile websites. Bad blood ensued; Lindsley, who came to the paper from the *Weekly Standard* at the recommendation of editor in chief (and Fox commentator) Bill Kristol, claimed he had been followed in Garrison by a Fox security man in a black Lincoln Navigator. Ailes said that it was a figment of his imagination. Lindsley had attended Notre Dame. Some suggested checking the Fox staff for other alumnae of the Fighting Irish. Perhaps it was a coincidence but one turned up: Muto, an associate producer of *The Factor*. Muto's electronic fingerprints were found on the video that had been posted on Gawker. He was so caught that he didn't even bother to deny it.

Muto's revelations put him in a small club of Fox whistleblowers. In 2001, Matt Gross, a junior figure at the Fox website, left the company. Two years later he charged that Fox reporters are lazy and that the network tries to provoke liberals and appeal to middle-aged white men. It is fair to say that the damage from those revelations was minimal. Gross is now an editor at *New York* magazine, a proudly progressive weekly.

In 1998, at a Fox affiliate in Tampa, two reporters, Jane Akre and her husband, Steve Wilson, prepared a series of reports on the agricultural biotechnology company Monsanto and its use of bovine growth hormone. The company protested, the reports were not shown, and the reporters were let go. They filed suit against Fox, and a jury decided against them on all counts except the question of whether they were legitimate whistle-blowers. An appellate court overturned that charge, and the two found themselves out of work but lionized by environmentalists—including Ailes's old friend Bobby Kennedy Jr.

Charlie Reina was a producer at Fox from 1997 to 2003 who, according to Brian Lewis, left after being told that he wouldn't be getting the promotion he expected. Reina blew the whistle on the daily memo sent by John Moody to Fox bureaus around the world. "To the newsroom personnel responsible for the channel's daytime programming, The Memo is the Bible," he told the Poynter Institute. "At the Fair and Balanced network everyone knows management's point of view, and in case they aren't sure how to get it on the air, The Memo is there to remind them." Reina was also the source of the information that Fox news reporters had been invited by management to refer to suicide bombers as "homicide bombers." Fox dismisses him as a disgruntled employee, and in any case, his charges didn't amount to much. Everyone already knew about the "homicide bomber" usage (it was right there on the air) and as for the daily memo, it revealed the not very shocking fact that the management of Fox News was involved in shaping the news coverage of Fox News. These days, Reina occasionally writes critical articles about Fox for the *Huffington Post*, although he hasn't been a source of any further scoops.

That's pretty much the extent of the leaks from Fox News. The Vatican has had more leaks in the past sixteen years. Of course, the pontiff believes in turning the other cheek. The head of Fox News does not.

As we boarded the plane, the Internet was buzzing with developments on the Muto case. Ailes was continuously updated by Brian Lewis, who stayed attached to his BlackBerry. Ailes regarded Fox's quick response as the first step of an effective deterrent action. The second step would be punishment. "He's probably sorry he ever tried this," said Lewis, to which Ailes muttered, "He will be by the time I get done with him."

Soon after I met Ailes, he told me about a lesson he had learned from Chet Collier: "Don't go out and shoot people. Just wait and they'll come by into your crosshairs. Then you squeeze the trigger."

Ailes revels in and works on his image as a badass. "In college, two buddies and I were drinking and we ran into a pack of frat boys," he told me one time. "We took them on, twelve to three, and they kicked the shit out of us." He has lots of stories like these, and he loves the bellicose picture they paint of him. When he first discovered e-mail he couldn't resist responding to nasty critics with offers to meet him in Manhattan and settle things like men. He offered to pay the airline ticket for one online heckler. "One way," he wrote. "You won't be going back." His staff eventually convinced him to give up the practice (as he subsequently attempted to convince an equally bellicose Rupert Murdoch to stay off Twitter).

It has been a long time since Ailes has had a physical fight, and he doesn't look like he could do much damage these days. But he is fond of recalling rougher times, like the night he punched a hole in the wall of an NBC control room where he was producing *The Tomorrow Show*. "It was just a drywall, and luckily I didn't hit any beams. But somebody put a frame around the hole and wrote, 'Don't mess with Roger Ailes.' I have my suspicions about who wrote that message. After all, if you have a reputation as a badass, you don't need to fight."

Ailes admits that he sometimes flies off the handle and, as he puts it, "creates bullshit." This can happen pretty much anywhere. Not long ago, on a ball field near his place in Garrison, his nephew accidentally hit a baseball through the window of a 2012 Prius parked in a church lot. The owners were Koreans who didn't speak much English, and they were extremely agitated. "It's just a damn window," Ailes told them. "I'll pay for the damn thing."

The owner was indignant. "We pray, you curse," he said.

"Fine," said Ailes. "Then let's *pray* over the fucking window. Maybe that'll fix it."

"It was a ten-minute incident that I turned into an hour," Ailes said when he told me the story. "Hell, it's lucky they didn't recognize me. It could have turned into a goddamn international scandal. But I *told* them I was sorry. . . ." He laughed. "Damn it, though, I was kind of glad that it was a Prius."

As he told the story, Ailes was already spinning it. "I do have a hair trigger, but I only use it on things that don't matter these days," he said. "I just do it to blow off steam, create some bullshit."

It recalled Ailes's boyhood awe at his father's volcanic anger. Perhaps Ailes was thinking of it, too. "I told Zac, 'Son, don't ever act like your father,'" he said. "And Zac said, 'Don't worry, I won't.'"

The other crisis du jour was an accusation by Newt Gingrich that Fox News' support for Mitt Romney was responsible for Gingrich's poor primary showing. Rick Santorum had made a similar claim when he dropped out of the race (Romney, on a visit to Ailes's office, had complained that Fox favored Gingrich and Santorum). Gingrich and Santorum had been Fox commentators before getting into the race and Ailes found their complaints self-serving and disloyal. Brian Lewis asked Ailes for guidance on how to respond to Newt. "Brush him back," Ailes said. "He's a sore loser and if he had won he would have been a sore winner."

Lewis nodded. Ailes was silent for a moment and then added, "Newt's a prick."

Lewis looked at his boss. They have been together for sixteen years and he has lasted because he is loyal and smart— smart enough, certainly, to know when an Ailes comment is better left unreported. "Doing PR for Fox News is like working on a permanent presidential campaign," Lewis told me.

The Fox public relations division is a marvel of speedy response and harsh, often ad hominem, replies to critics. "I don't start fights," Ailes likes to say, "but I do counterpunch." Some of those punches land below the belt. When the University of Maryland published its survey alleging that Fox viewers are misinformed, Michael Clemente responded by noting that the university had been ranked by the *Princeton Review* as one of the schools whose students do the least studying, and as the nation's best party campus. "Given these fine academic distinctions, we'll regard the study with the same level of veracity it was researched with," Clemente said. More recently, Fairleigh Dickinson University published a poll purporting to show that Fox viewers were chronically uninformed. A spokesman for Fox answered, "Considering FDU's undergraduate school is ranked as one of the worst in the country, we suggest the school invest in improving its weak academic program instead of spending money on frivolous polling—their student body does not deserve to be so ill-informed."

Ailes took the same hard-line tack in dealing with the complaints of Santorum and Gingrich. "Santorum lost his Senate seat in Pennsylvania by seventeen points," he said. "I suppose Fox was responsible for that. And Newt was in Congress all those years and just about none of his fellow congressmen are supporting him. That's supposed to be my fault, too?"

Ailes had inflamed his enemies on the left by hiring Santorum, Gingrich, Mike Huckabee—and especially Sarah Palin—as commentators. Some critics charged that he was trying to buy up all the candidates for the presidency. The accusation rankled him because it was so obviously amateurish—an example of journalists who don't know politics trying to impute dumb motives to him. "I knew when I hired them they weren't viable candidates," Ailes told me. "Huckabee couldn't raise a dime for a campaign. Evan Bayh [a former Democratic senator from Indiana now on Fox] has a better chance to be nominated." He publicly said that he had hired Palin because he knew she had no chance to be nominated. Palin fired back with a statement of her own: "I wonder if he is aware that the same thing was said about me when I ran for city council, mayor, and eventually governor." Palin was still on the Fox payroll and Ailes decided later that week to placate her with a clarification—he had merely been referring to 2012.

When Palin first went to work for Fox, there had been righteous outrage at many of the other networks—here was another example of Ailes turning Fox into an annex (or the center) of the GOP. In fact, almost everyone wanted Palin; she had, according to a Fox insider, offers from CNN, CBS, and ABC. Now there were rumors, sparked by a recent appearance on NBC's *Today Show*, that she was headed to the Peacock Network.

Ailes was untroubled by this. For one thing, it was far from certain that he wanted to keep her: Palin is an expensive commentator; Fox had helped build a studio equipped with a state-of-the-art camera, and a satellite, in her Alaska home. When I asked Ailes, somewhere over Kentucky, if he was angry at Palin's appearance on *Today*, he shook his head. "She

couldn't have done *The Today Show* without my permission,"
he explained. "We have a contract." Ailes had agreed because
he knew that if she did well on *Today* (which most critics
thought she had) it would strengthen the journalistic cred of
one of Fox's star commentators. Allowing her to go on *Today*
meant that the show owed him a favor. And the rumor that
she might defect to NBC put pressure on ABC, whose *Good
Morning America* was trying to displace *Today*'s long-standing
hold on first place in the morning. For Ailes it was win-win-
win, a three-cushion bank shot. And, as a bonus, Palin had to
be wondering how much Ailes actually wanted her and what,
when her contract expired, he would be willing to pay.

■ ■ ■

The flight to Chapel Hill took an hour and twenty minutes,
and Ailes spent most of the time looking over typed notes for
his speech. He had been working on it for some time, and
using visitors as sounding boards for the remarks he intended
to make. A few weeks earlier, a delegation of students from
the Industrial College of the Armed Forces had come to see
him at Fox. These were Ailes's kind of students—officers just
breaking into the senior ranks, dressed in suits, sporting neat
haircuts, and with respectful manners. They were there to
hear his views on a subject they were studying: how to ensure
that the news media enhance national security.

"Good luck with that one," said Ailes with a laugh. "That'll
be a new role for 'em." He was in his customary place at the
head of the table with his tie undone and his suit jacket
thrown over the back of his chair. The officers stared at him
keenly, as if this was their first brush with cynicism. But he
knew exactly who they were. He meets with groups almost
every day, and he doesn't like surprises. He had scanned the
bios of the officers. Only two had spent time at Ivy League

schools, a telltale liberal credential to Ailes. The rest, he assumed, would be more or less sympathetic. Still, he wanted to make it clear that he had no apologies to make. After running through some of the statistics on Fox's supremacy, he said, "We have our detractors, but they are always people we are beating. I don't let it hurt my feelings. We are fair and balanced here. We always cover the news. We give Obama crap—that's our job. When Bush was in, we gave him crap, showing pictures of Abu Ghraib and so on. We make mistakes sometimes and we correct 'em right away, but we have never had to take a story down, like the *New York Times*, CBS, and CNN." It was a random selection: Ailes has a very detailed list of the self-inflicted humiliations of his mainstream competitors.

"Sir, when is it justified to ask the media to hold off on news for national security reasons?" a future brigadier asked.

"I have no problem delaying news when national security is involved," said Ailes. "I respect the public's right to know, but it's moronic to say there are *never* extenuating circumstances." To illustrate, he recounted the time when two Fox journalists were captured by Palestinian terrorists and held hostage in Gaza for thirteen days. Ailes had given the order to Fox News people to mention the capture but not to discuss it. He made a similar request to the other networks, and they complied. "The terrorists were holding rifles to our guys' heads, trying to make them convert to Islam or some damn thing," Ailes said. "One of our guys was gay, and his partner wanted to go on the air and ask the terrorists to let him go. Shit, that would have been good, right? Our guy would have had a whole new problem over there. So yeah, I'm not a neutral when people's lives are at stake."

There were enthusiastic nods around the table. Ailes was now on a roll. In quick order he pronounced green cars a waste of time ("I'll buy one when they can make 'em comfortable, affordable, and cost effective"), denounced the American educational system ("Iceland beats us in math scores! Iceland, what the hell is that? Four people?"), sneered at his former employer, NBC ("I told them not to name the cable channel MSNBC. MS is a damn disease"), and explained that citizen journalism is mostly crap ("These days even real reporters almost never abide by the normal rules of journalism, let alone so-called citizen journalists").

"A lot of kids go into journalism because they want to change the world, or they want to get invited to Washington cocktail parties," Ailes said. "Those are lousy reasons. That's not what this job is all about, being on good terms with the people in power or the people you agree with. They put one story critical of something the president is doing on the air and they think it covers them, that they're doing their job. Bullshit."

The officers didn't know it at the time, and neither did I, but Ailes had been rehearsing his message to the journalism students of North Carolina.

■ ■ ■

We were fifteen minutes from landing in North Carolina when Ailes put down his notes and asked Brian Lewis what was going on in the world. "Newt is saying that Fox is less conservative than CNN," Lewis reported. Ailes laughed. "Newt's auditioning for a job over there. He's going to need one, because he's sure as hell not getting one with us again."

Lewis read Ailes a summary of the flap over Democratic operative Hilary Rosen's comment that Ann Romney, mother of five, had never worked a day in her life. Ailes spun it without hesitation. "Obama's the one who never worked a day in his life. He never earned a penny that wasn't public money.

How many fund-raisers does he attend every week? How often does he play basketball and golf? I wish *I* had that kind of time. He's lazy, but the media won't report that." He noticed my arched eyebrows and added, "*I* didn't come up with that. Obama said that, to Barbara Walters." (What Obama said was that he feels a laziness in himself that he attributes to his laid-back upbringing in Hawaii.)

Talk turned to the trial, due to start that day in Chapel Hill, of former senator and vice presidential candidate John Edwards. Edwards was accused of having illegally used campaign funds to support his mistress, Rielle Hunter. The amounts were relatively small, and I wondered aloud why a man as rich as Edwards would have taken that kind of risk.

"A married man who gives money to another woman can't very well take it out of the joint account," Ailes observed drily.

A car was waiting for us when we deplaned. On the way to the Carolina Inn, a charming hotel on campus, Lewis briefed Ailes for a last time on what to expect. The dean of the school, Susan King, was a TV journalist whom Ailes knew from the old days at CNBC. "She's a nice lady," Ailes said. "Probably a liberal, but pleasant." He had done his own research on the faculty of the journalism school. "Eleven to one, liberals. Well, that's not as bad as some of them."

After check-in, Lewis and Jimmy, the security guy, went to the auditorium for a run-through. Ailes and I adjourned to the restaurant, where, over Carolina-style pulled pork sandwiches and fries, he talked about what he saw as the emerging Democratic charge that Republicans were waging a war on women. There had been reporting in the last couple of days that Romney was trailing the president by 7 percent among female voters. Ailes has been reading polls for more than forty years, and he wasn't impressed. "They're calling it

a gender gap to make Romney look vulnerable," he said.
"What they don't say is in the same poll Romney is leading
among male voters. Why isn't that a gender gap? What's the
difference?"

It is Ailes's natural tendency, as a Republican in a Democratic media environment, to turn things upside down. Are
white males overwhelmingly for Romney? Fine, what is the
percentage of black males supporting Obama? Is the Affordable Care Act imperiled because four conservatives on the
Supreme Court vote as a bloc? Okay, how will the liberal bloc
vote? Is the Tea Party polarizing? Maybe the other pole is
equally at fault. Since the advent of Fox News, there is a television network that frames these stories from a conservative
perspective. "We'll report on the gender gap from both sides,"
Ailes said. "The other networks aren't even aware that there
is another side."

Ailes expects that Romney will be treated unfairly by the
mainstream media in the coming campaign, especially in the
debates. "Mitt is a lot tougher than he looks," says Ailes.
"There were eight guys in the forest when the primaries
started, and he's the one who came out alive. But in debates,
reporters never ask Republican candidates about foreign policy, the economy, or energy. They ask, 'Do you think Jesus
lives in the sky?' If I were him, I'd hire [Florida congressman]
Allen West to play Obama in prep. West's smart, he knows all
the liberal positions, and he's black. Be a good chance for
Mitt to get used to being called a racist."

We were on a second cup of coffee when Brian and Jimmy
returned from their inspection tour. Jimmy reported that security for the event would be handled by the university. Heck-
lers would be asked politely to desist, and if they didn't, they'd
be escorted out. In fact, Ailes is very rarely challenged in public (and he wasn't that day), but he didn't want to leave any-

thing to chance. Neither did university authorities, who stationed cops around the building. To Ailes, who remembers the sixties without nostalgia, elite universities are forever enemy territory.

"If I get a job application from someone who went to Princeton or Harvard, they have a harder time selling me. I'd rather hire state school kids," Ailes once told me. "They hustle, they're not entitled, and they have a work ethic, a desire to win, and practical intelligence." This, of course, describes Roger Ailes, son of Warren G. Harding High School and Ohio University, but it is far from a universal truth (I speak as the product of public education). In fact, Fox News is rife with graduates of fancy schools. John Moody, the first executive vice president for news, is a Cornell man. Woody Fraser attended Dartmouth. The Washington bureau includes Harvard grads Jennifer Griffin, Catherine Herridge, Chris Wallace, Charles Krauthammer (who went to Harvard Medical school and also attended Oxford), and Bill Kristol. Lou Dobbs of FBN is a Harvard grad, too. John Stossel, Judy Miller, and Andrew Napolitano have degrees from Princeton. Dick Morris, Gerri Willis (MBA), and Steve Hayes (Law School) are Columbia alums. Foreign correspondent Steve Harrigan has a PhD from Yale. Amy Kellogg matriculated at Brown and holds a master's degree from Stanford. Business reporter Brenda Buttner is not only a Harvard woman but also a Rhodes scholar. Commentator Charles Lane has degrees from both Harvard *and* Yale. And this is just a partial list. Ailes's suspicion of the corrosive effects of an elite American education notwithstanding, Fox's journalists don't seem to have been permanently damaged by their exposure to liberal ideas. If anything, it gives Fox an advantage over the competition. Very few network news organizations are staffed with graduates of right-leaning schools such as Hillsdale Col-

lege, Liberty University, or the service academies; and they
therefore often lack an accurate picture of what the plurality
of Americans who identify as conservatives are actually thinking about, or interested in.

■ ■ ■

That night, Ailed faced his audience dressed in his customary
black business suit, looking happy and well rested. After our
lunch he had taken a long nap. There were twin beds in his
hotel room, and he invited me to join him. I was tempted—
being able to say that I had slept with Roger Ailes in North
Carolina was almost irresistible—but I declined on the
grounds that it would be inhumane to submit him to my snor-
ing. And so he had slumbered away the afternoon undis-
turbed, arrived at Carroll Hall full of energy, and immediately
lit into the crowd. "I understand most of you are journalism
students, is that correct? All right. Well, I think you ought to
change your major, because you're probably all interested in
politics and you probably are going into journalism because
you think you can affect politics. Well, maybe you can, maybe
you can't. But if you're going in to affect it, you have to think
about that, because you might want to go to political science
where you can join a campaign, help elect who you want,
push the issues you believe in."

The audience murmured, but no one protested. North Carolina is a fine university but it is also in the South, where
young people are taught to respect their elders. Besides, Ailes
was paying them the compliment of being blunt, which made
him interesting.

Ailes told the room that the job of the press is to act as "a
watchdog. Not a lapdog or an attack dog, but as a watchdog."
He went on, "If you want to bring world peace or save starv-
ing children, both very noble goals, the way to effect that as a

journalist is to investigate why the United Nations is so inef-
fective at doing either of those." Ailes does not care for the
UN, and Fox had aggressively reported on its failures, most
notably the corruption in its Oil-for-Food scandal. "I was at a
UN party and a man I don't know came up to me and said,
'What you are doing on Oil-for-Food is very, very dangerous to
you and your family,'" Ailes recalls. He didn't learn the man's
identity, but Fox security, never lax, was alerted. Before his
speech in North Carolina, Ailes had informed Dean Susan
King that as the head of a news network, he would have to
steer clear of politics. But he nudged up against it. President
Obama was developing a strategy of blaming the recession on
big capital and demanding that "millionaires and billionaires"
pay more taxes.

"Every time I needed a job, I had to go to a rich guy," Ailes
said. "I love the poor guy; he had no job. I got a job. I tried to
help the poor, okay? But I'm not going to let anybody divide
me against the people who actually gave me the jobs. That
does not seem very productive." Now, of course, he is the mil-
lionaire with the jobs. He told the students that under his
stewardship, Fox had experienced fifty-eight straight quarters
of growth, been the number one cable news network for 123
consecutive months, and is the only television news operation
never to have laid anyone off for financial reasons. Here was
news a keen journalism student could use. Only Fox and
Bloomberg, of the national electronic media, were fertile
sources of employment.

Ailes didn't want to leave an impression that he is a heartless plutocrat. "I'm not a big fan of government confiscating
more than a third of what we make," he said. "I think a third's
fair." By this time, he was detached from the notes he had
carefully prepared and was winging it. He praised Martin Luther King Jr. for his nonviolence and American soldiers for

their willingness to fight and die for their country, without noticing any contradiction. He admonished the students to remember that America is a country that people try to get into, not escape from. He said that he believes in climate change ("every time you go outside it changes") but that man-made global warming was unproven and environmentalists "keep trying to change the climate for God." At one point he blanked on the name of CNN anchor Soledad O'Brien and referred to her as "the girl named after the prison." When the talk ended, the kids applauded politely and some lined up for a photo.

On the way back to the airport in a university SUV, Brian Lewis read Ailes reactions to his remarks, which had been tweeted by reporters in the audience. Ailes seemed amused by how quickly his every word had been disseminated. He was pleased by how it had gone, although he regretted the Soledad O'Brien reference.

Lewis then began summarizing reactions from the mole story, which had been a major topic of conversation all day in the media and on the Internet. Most of the accounts, Ailes thought, were fair and balanced, even sympathetic to Fox. "Nobody likes a rat," Ailes said.

"I don't see how a guy could be so disloyal to his own friends and employer," said Jimmy, who had been silent for most of the day. "I just don't get that."

"Gawker paid him five thousand dollars for the stuff he leaked," said Lewis.

"Five thousand dollars?" Ailes, who was sitting in the front seat, sounded incredulous. A man had committed profes-sional suicide for five grand?

"You know," said Jimmy, whose career in the NYPD was spent investigating organized crime and drug dealers, "if this

Gawker paid for stolen goods, it could be part of the crime, same as if somebody hires a hit man."

There was a pause and then Ailes said to Brian, "We should have legal look into that." A few weeks later, the New York district attorney's office sent detectives to seize Joe Muto's files and notebooks. Muto tweeted that he was suspected of grand larceny. Fox also let it be known that it was contemplat-ing a suit against Gawker, which would, at a minimum, cost the online publisher a lot of money, and perhaps serve as a deterrent to similar Judas-like betrayals.

Ailes settled back in his seat, and we drove through the Carolina night. He had met the enemy and they were his.

CHAPTER SIXTEEN

ZAC'S BOX

On May 15, 2012, Roger Ailes turned seventy-two and received a birthday gift from his greatest rival. CNN's prime-time shows registered their lowest ratings in fifteen years. In the nine o'clock hour, Hannity outpaced Piers Morgan in the key age demographic of twenty-five to fifty-four by almost ten to one. It was a victory of epic proportions, which Ailes, Beth, and Zac celebrated with a homemade birthday cake.

Not long ago, oil tycoon T. Boone Pickens asked Ailes if he is a billionaire. He isn't. He works for a living, like his old man did at the Packard factory. That is the way he sees himself, and the way he wants to be seen. "I haven't ever really had much time for introspection," he told me. "My life has been mostly about being presented with hard problems and solving them, doing what needs to be done." These have been other people's problems. At the Douglas show, "get Ailes" (to fix things) became a crisis-management mantra. He saved the televised Nixon from himself in 1968, showed Ronald Reagan how to protect himself from the ravages of old age on the debate stage in 1988, and produced an ad campaign that enabled George H. W. Bush's come-from-behind victory in 1988. Corporate CEOs and political aspirants paid him handsomely for troubleshooting and image making. And, finally, Ailes breathed life and vigor (and undreamed-of profitability) into Rupert Murdoch's hunch that a vast number of Americans wanted a different sort of television news.

Ailes's contract expires in June 2013, and he fully intends to keep on going at Fox News.* The division of News Corp into two companies complicated the negotiation. Fox Entertainment, which includes Ailes's domain, is by far the larger and more lucrative, and Ailes wanted to see that expressed in stock as well as salary. Ten months before the target date, he wasn't sure that he and Murdoch would come to terms. "I'm happy where I am, and this year our profit is very close to a billion dollars," he said. "But if they can find somebody else who can produce that way, okay, I'll find another job."

Ailes is infuriated by press reports that he has no succession plan. "Of course I have one," he told me. "I would be a very irresponsible executive not to. I don't know if they will be implemented—that's not up to me. But the ideas are on paper, and they'll be there when I go."

Some people think his legacy may be transient. "When you leave, you leave the keys," Jack Welch says. "If Rupert leaves too, and a left-leaning Murdoch comes in, it could change a lot of things."

---

* In October 2012, he signed a four-year contract with a very substantial raise.

Ailes agrees that new ownership could make a radical shift, but he finds it highly unlikely.

"Fox News is built on the principle of fair and balanced. An owner who gets away from that would kill it."

That isn't likely to happen. Fox News is not just a network; it is an entirely new approach to the news, and its impact goes well beyond the confines of the network. "Not only has Roger changed the way television is done, he has imbued an entire generation of producers with his vision," says Neil Cavuto. One of them, David Rhodes, who spent twelve years as an Ailes protégé, is now the president of CBS News. And that is just the beginning. The old network pose of "news from no-where," which disguised a homogeneous worldview and story selection cribbed from the front page of the *New York Times*, still exists, but even Ailes concedes that the networks are far more fair-minded than they once were.

"Roger took some charisma and great ideas for shows and worked magic—framing the news in terms that are favorable to the Republicans," says Rachel Maddow. "I feel that he has won. If the media were left of center before, they aren't now."

Some respected liberal media figures like Maddow, Bill Keller, Eric Deggans, and Mark Danner lament this. But a surprising number think that Fox News, by breaking the old monopoly on the news, is a positive development. "Roger gets a bum rap when people say that his network is biased, shallow, and bad for the country," says Rick Kaplan, who has run both CNN and MSNBC.

Whatever Ailes's professional legacy, he remains a realist about the cult of personality that has grown up around him at Fox. "Right now, everybody thinks I'm the greatest guy in the world," he says. "I'm sure you heard that a lot. The eulogies will be great, but people will be stepping over my body before

it gets cold. Within a day or two, everybody will be complaining about what a prick I was and all the things I didn't do for
them." He seemed proud of the cynicism. He always does
when he is trying to sound hard-boiled.

■ ■ ■

One of the first things I noticed about Roger Ailes is that he
has a very acute sense of his own mortality. "I'd give anything
for another ten years," he often says, and typically, he has
crunched the numbers.

"My doctor told me that I'm old, fat, and ugly, but none of
those things is going to kill me immediately," he told me
shortly before his seventy-second birthday. "The actuaries say
I have six to eight years. The best tables give me ten. Three
thousand days, more or less."

I asked if he is afraid to die. "Because of my hemophilia,
I've been prepared to face death all of my life," he told me.
"As a boy I spent a lot of time in hospitals. My parents had to
leave at the end of visiting hours, and I spent a lot of time
just lying there in the dark, thinking about the fact that any
accident could be dangerous or even fatal. So, I'm ready. Everybody fears the unknown. But I have a strong feeling
there's something bigger than us. I don't think all this exists
because some rocks happened to collide. I'm at peace. When
it comes, I'll be fine, calm. I'll miss life, though. Especially
my family."

One day in his office, Ailes showed me a photo of Zac in a
school play. The boy was made up as Teddy Roosevelt, in a
suit and a fake mustache. Ailes studied the picture wistfully.
The most painful fact of Ailes's life is that he isn't likely to see
his son as a grown man. "I never really knew much about my
father's life, what it was really like," he says. "I'm not going to

be here forever and I want Zac to know me." Recently, he and
Beth took Zac, now twelve, back to Warren on a sentimental
journey that included dinner with old school friends. "One of
the girls there told Zac that I was one of the cool kids," Ailes
said with evident pride. "Don't know what the hell he made of
that."

Since Zac was four, Ailes has been putting things away for
him in memory boxes; there are now nine, stuffed with me-
mentos, personal notes, photos, and messages from Ailes to
his son. They are meant to be opened when Ailes is gone. I
was curious to see what Ailes was leaving behind. He was re-
luctant to show me, but he finally brought one of the boxes
to his office. I had been expecting an ornate trunk, but it
turned out to be nothing more than a large plastic container
stuffed with what appeared to be a random assortment of
memorabilia. There was a pocket-size copy of the U.S. Constitution in which Ailes wrote, "The founders believed it and
so should you"; photos of Zac and Beth on family vacations;
an itinerary of their trip to the White House Christmas
party; and a sentimental fourteenth-anniversary card from
Beth ("It's important for him to know that his mommy loved
his daddy," Ailes said) on which he had scrawled a note to
Zac: "Your mother is a beautiful woman. Always take care of
her." I saw a printed program from a Fourth of July celebration in Garrison in which father and son read patriotic texts
aloud, articles and press releases about Ailes's career, and a
couple of biographies of Ronald Reagan. Tossed in with the
other stuff was a plain brown envelope that contained $2,000
in cash and a note: "Here's the allowance I owe you," which
Ailes said was an inside joke sure to make his son smile.
There were also a few symbolic gold coins, "just in case everything goes to hell," he told me. "If you have a little gold
and a handgun, you can always get across the Canadian bor-

der." Zac is still too young for a pistol, but he sometimes accompanies his father to the shooting range at West Point for target practice.

At the bottom of the box there was a copy of Sun Tzu's *The Art of War* with paternal advice inscribed on the first page:

> Z—
>
> Avoid war if at all possible but never give up your freedom—or your honor. Always stand for what is right.
>
> If absolutely FORCED to fight, then fight with courage and win. Don't try to win . . . win!
>
> Love,
> Dad

Courage. Honor. Freedom. This is a note that could have been written by Rudyard Kipling or Teddy Roosevelt to their sons, a celebration of manly virtues that have long since ceased to be fashionable. They are the virtues Ailes learned in his hardscrabble boyhood in small-town Ohio, and they are what he believes in today; they are the simple residue of a very complicated life.

"This is advice Zac might need to hear from me in ten years and I won't be here to give it to him," Ailes said as he closed the box. "I've told him, if he has a problem or he feels he needs me, to go off to a quiet place and listen, and he will hear my voice."

I asked Roger Ailes what he imagined heaven would be like. "I'm pretty sure that God's got a sense of humor," he said. "I think he gets a laugh out of me from time to time, so I suppose things will be all right."

"What if you get there and it turns out that God is a liberal?" I asked.

Ailes paused. It was something that evidently hadn't occurred to him. "Well, hell, if God's a liberal, that's his business," he said. He paused again, imagining it. "But I doubt very much that he is. He's got a good heart." Ailes sat back, pleased with his moment of theological speculation. The hell with his critics here on earth. He has every expectation that when the time comes, he will find himself standing at the seat of judgment before a fair and balanced God.

ELECTION NIGHT

I arrived at Fox News on election night, around seven, and was ushered into the sports suite on the second floor of the News Corp building. About two hundred network executives and invited guests mingled in the bar area or grazed at a buffet featuring sushi and grilled lamb on skewers. The men wore business suits, the women evening attire. Mounted along a long wall of the rectangular room were eight large television screens offering a choice of election coverage: Fox News, Fox Business, Fox Broadcasting, and the competition— CNN, MSNBC, and the major networks. From time to time someone glanced up at the TV screens, but it was too early for actual results and, anyway, the volume was turned down so low that you had to concentrate to hear the talking heads over the murmur of the cocktail hour.

Thirty feet away from the crowd, directly in front of the screens, Roger Ailes, wearing his customary black suit, sat at a round coffee table staring intently at the screens. Half a dozen empty chairs were arranged in a crescent on either side. "These are reserved," a Fox News staffer told me. It was an explanation, not an invitation to sit down, but when the aide turned her back, I slipped into a chair next to him. "Our electoral map is too small," he told me by way of greeting. There was a phone on the table with direct lines to every department of the network, from engineering and security to the anchor desk and the decision room. Ailes pressed a button, said a few words, and watched the map almost instantaneously grow. "That's better," he said. "Right now it doesn't matter, but it will when the results start coming in. Look how small CNN's is. Who the hell wants to look at a map that you can barely see?"

This was the eleventh election night since Ailes helped put Richard Nixon in the White House, his fifth presiding over Fox News. The public polls were a virtual tie, but I figured if anyone had inside info, it would be Ailes. "I guess you're expecting a late night," I ventured.

"Could be," said Ailes. It sounded like a late night was the last thing he was looking forward to.

"What are your exit polls showing?"

Ailes shrugged. He doesn't believe much in exit polls, and he is skeptical of even his own in-house experts. That day, at lunch, Karl Rove had told him he thought Romney would win. "Hell, maybe Karl's right," he said. "We'll see."

As the 8:00 p.m. poll closings approached, the crescent around Ailes began to fill in. Beth sat on his right, intermittently editing the front page of the *Putnam County News and Recorder* on her iPad and occasionally briefing Roger on developments in Garrison. The room itself was getting quieter in anticipation of the first results when suddenly there was a rustling at the door—Rupert Murdoch, accompanied by a small entourage. Ailes hit the button to the decision room for an update; he had it by the time Murdoch wended his way through the room and sat down. He gave Ailes a comradely pat on the back and asked, "What does it look like?"

"Ohio, Florida, Virginia, and North Carolina are all too close to call," said Ailes.

Murdoch threw up his hands in a you-just-told-me-what-everyone-in-America-already-knows gesture. "Well, what do *you* think?"

"Too early to tell," Ailes said. "Could go either way."

"Roger is always a pessimist," Murdoch proclaimed to no one in particular. Bill Shine came by with news. Jeb Bush had just tweeted that Florida was looking good. A couple of counties were unexpectedly strong.

"Jeb wouldn't have tweeted this if he wasn't sure," said someone. "He must know something." Heads nodded in affirmation. Ailes leaned over and instructed Shine to find out exactly what counties Jeb was talking about.

Meanwhile, the screens weren't providing much in the way of enlightenment. Obama and Romney were each winning the states they were supposed to win. The swing states were all still swinging. From time to time Ailes called down to the decision room, but came up with nothing new. It was all on the air. Aside from enlarging the map and contacting engineering when he saw a technical glitch during an interview with Robert Gibbs, Ailes was a spectator. "Moody and Clemente are solid news guys," he said. "There's no reason for me to get involved."

Of course, Ailes had been very much involved since the primaries, the guiding force at the only Republican-leaning source of television news. Obama, who appeared on every TV show from Jimmy Fallon to *The View*, had declined a standing invitation to appear on Fox. Ailes, in the Nixon campaign,

had more or less invented the strategy of keeping his candidate away from critical interviews; he understood perfectly
well why the president had preferred chatting with Whoopi
Goldberg and David Letterman to a session with Bill O'Reilly
or Chris Wallace. A few days before the election, the Pew Research Center for the People and the Press published a survey
that found just 6 percent of Fox's coverage of the president
had been positive, 46 percent negative, a ratio of 8–1.
(MSNBC, Fox's chief cable rival, was far more partisan—only
3 percent of its Romney coverage was positive, 71 percent
negative, a ratio of 23–1. The broadcast network coverage
came out mildly pro-Obama, but far less than it had been in
2008.)

But if Fox had rooted for Romney during the campaign, it
was dispassionate and professional. The young talent Ailes
had chosen and developed—Megyn Kelly, Bret Baier, Shep
Smith, Ed Henry, and others—were fair and balanced without quotation marks. Earlier that day, Ailes had chaired what
is known as the exit poll meeting, a gathering of the anchors
and commentators scheduled to appear that night. It was a bipartisan group and Ailes cautioned them all to stay positive
and energetic. "If the candidate you like isn't doing well, don't
look like somebody just ran over your dog," he said. In the
event, Fox was among the first networks to call the election
for the president, and when Karl Rove objected that the decision to award Obama Ohio—and, essentially the election—
was premature, Kelly marched down the hallway and
confronted Arnon Mishkin, the head of the decision team.
"You tell me if you stand by your call in Ohio," she demanded.
Mishkin stood by the call, and he was right. It was the most
dramatic television moment of the evening, underscoring
Ailes's contention that Fox was a reliable source of news (and

in the process removing the modifier "rising" from Megyn Kelly's stardom).

It was apparent long before the Ohio call that this wasn't going to be Romney's night. When someone in the crescent groaned at the loss of Pennsylvania, Ailes said, "Hey, it's early. The second day at the Alamo didn't look that good, either." He paused, considering the implications of that observation, and barked out a laugh. "Hell, maybe that's not the best example. The Alamo didn't turn out too well in the end."

Wisconsin came in, for Obama. "That's one Romney should have won," Ailes said. Murdoch got up to mingle, and he was replaced in the crescent by Jack Keane, the retired general who helped convince George W. Bush to launch the successful troop surge in Iraq and now serves as a Fox military analyst. "This thing is far from over," he said in a pronounced New York accent. He said it with the certainty of a man used to command, but he couldn't change what people were seeing on the screen, and already the crescent was bubbling with recriminations. "Chris Christie's name should be in the dictionary next to the definition of the word 'traitor,'" said a woman who was angry at the New Jersey governor for the electoral boost he had given Obama when he embraced the president in the aftermath of Hurricane Sandy (later that night, on MSNBC, Chris Matthews expressed his gratitude for the hurricane and the help it had given the president's image). Others blamed the auto bailout, the American education system, or the voters. A woman from Tennessee said the real problem was the welfare state. "My family came from nothing," she said, "and we worked for what we have. Nobody wants to work anymore. They're just looking for handouts."

Ailes looked up from the screen and frowned. "I don't know about that," he said. "About ten percent of the population really needs help. We should *quadruple* their aid or they'll never get out of poverty. Instead, we keep them at subsistence level and give the entitlement money to people who don't really need it." The woman gave Ailes an uncomprehending nod.

Nobody, I noticed, had a good word to say about Romney, a man who had, at the very least, campaigned hard on their party's behalf. I admit to a moment of petty satisfaction at the cold shoulder he was getting. Romney and I are the same age and we grew up near one another in Michigan. He was the governor's son, handsome, rich, and famous. I was none of those things. In high school I fell for a classmate who, alas, had a huge crush on Mitt Romney, whom she knew from Sunday school. Fifty years is a minute when it comes to unrequited teenage romance.

Rupert Murdoch came by, said he was hearing good things about Virginia, and what did Roger know? Ailes checked with the decision desk and reported that the Richmond precincts were in, which *might* be construed as good news. Murdoch got the message. Once more he patted Roger on the shoulder, and then he left.

A young man wearing a black cowboy hat and western boots joined the crescent. He was introduced as John Rich, half of the country duo Big & Rich. He was the only showbiz figure at the party, and he seemed optimistic. "I've been out singing for Mitt for weeks," he said. "He's got a good chance, right?"

"He'd have to draw to an inside straight," Ailes said. "Virginia, Florida, Ohio, North Carolina . . ." Rich blinked. Maybe he didn't know so much about politics, but he evidently knows poker. He wasn't likely to be singing at the inauguration.

We watched Nevada, a state that led the nation in housing foreclosures, fall to Obama. Hispanics made the difference. "When this election is over, I'm going to give a speech," Ailes told me. "Conservatives aren't going to like it but I don't give a damn. There is a confusion between the issue of sovereignty and the issue of immigration. Of course we have to protect our sovereignty and the border. But we've got to stop insulting millions of people by calling them 'illegal aliens' and acting like hopping the fence to feed your kids is a capital crime. We need to give them a way to enter legally, contribute, and feel welcome." He knew that right-wing ideologues, led by his friend Rush Limbaugh, would insist that the GOP had underperformed because it had been insufficiently hard-line, and that the party had to double down. But Ailes was making a different bet. The GOP was going to need candidates who didn't come across as heartless plutocrats or anti-Latino xenophobes and who had a less doctrinaire interpretation of core conservative principles. This wasn't an election-night epiphany; Ailes had said similar things to me over the previous few months. But it was time to turn thought into action. The next day, at a production meeting with the senior staff, Ailes reiterated his views in very strong terms. Barely twenty-four hours later, Sean Hannity—the hardest of hard-liners on illegal immigration—would experience a change of heart, or as he put it, an evolution in his thinking: "If people are here, law abiding, participating for years, their kids are born here, you know, first secure the border, then the pathway to citizenship."

Around 10:40 p.m., Ailes put in a last call to the decision desk. He asked some questions about key counties in several unsettled swing states, listened impassively, and replaced the receiver. He had been hunched over the coffee table for hours without so much as a bathroom break. Now he signaled to Beth that it was time to go home. "You can stay here until tomorrow," he said to the few true believers still in the crescent, "but I'm leaving. I want to kiss Zac good night before he goes to sleep."

As we rode the elevator down to the deserted lobby, Ailes seemed to be in remarkably good spirits. During his consulting days he had won elections and lost elections and he knew that in American politics there are no final victories or defeats. A second Obama term was not a disaster. Hell, looked at in a certain way, it was an opportunity. Earlier that evening, Bob Beckel had stopped by to offer Ailes a few words of mock condolence over the Obama trend, but Ailes declined to be baited. "If Romney wins, it's good for the taxpayers," he said. "If Obama wins, it's great for our ratings." Barack Obama had four more years, but so did Roger Ailes, and he intended to use them to grow Fox News ever bigger (that night, as it turned out, Fox got the highest prime-time ratings in its history); build the number one business channel on cable (if Rupert will just give him a hundred million dollars for distribution); and showcase Republican candidates and policies that couldn't be dismissed as nativist or elitist. All that would start bright and early the next morning. If there is a first principle in the world of Roger Ailes, after fifty years spent at the heart of American politics and entertainment, it is this: No matter what the hell else happens, the goddamn show must go on.

ACKNOWLEDGMENTS

I want to thank Sentinel Books, starting with its preternaturally smart publisher, Adrian Zackheim, my gifted editor, Niki Papadopoulos, and the talented Natalie Horbachevsky. They are real pros whose contributions to this book have been invaluable.

I am grateful, as always, to my agent, Flip Brophy. I'm lucky to have her and I know it.

Many thanks to Julia Kardon for her meticulous fact checking, and to Nephi Tyler, who did a terrific job as my editorial assistant/researcher, and to my first reader, my son, Coby, who is blessed with great taste and unwavering (sometimes brutal) intellectual honesty.

A lot of people took the time to talk to me for this book. Many are quoted, others have preferred to stay off the record. I appreciate everyone's help and generosity.

I am indebted to Brian Lewis, Fox News executive vice president for corporate communications, who was always willing to answer just one more question; and to Ailes's assistants, Gina Dell 'Aquila and Liz Downey, who were consistently cheerful and helpful.

Special thanks goes to Judy Laterza, Roger Ailes's longtime executive assistant, who handled my many requests with generous efficiency and exceptional kindness.

INDEX